Big Book of Monthly Arts & Crafts
Preschool–Kindergarten

Table of Contents

About This Book

Big Book of Monthly Arts & Crafts
Preschool–Kindergarten

Whatever the season, you'll find just the arts-and-crafts activity you are looking for in this resource compiled of the best ideas from the Monthly Arts and Crafts series! For each month, we have included a collection of one-of-a-kind arts-and-crafts activities to add spark to your monthly thematic plans and ignite creativity in your little ones. Each activity includes a brief introduction to a theme, a quick and easy materials list, simple step-by-step instructions, a full-color illustration, and one or more teaching tips to help the activity go smoothly. Both teacher tested and kid approved, these arts-and-crafts activities will provide a year's worth of creative fun!

In every apple near and far
Is a happy little star!

Managing Editor: Allison E. Ward

Editorial Team: Becky S. Andrews, Kimberley Bruck, Karen P. Shelton, Diane Badden, Elizabeth H. Lindsay, Susan Walker, Karen A. Brudnak, Sarah Hamblet, Hope Rodgers, Dorothy C. McKinney

Production Team: Lisa K. Pitts, Ivy L. Koonce (COVER ARTIST), Pam Crane, Clevell Harris, Rebecca Saunders, Jennifer Tipton Bennett, Chris Curry, Theresa Lewis Goode, Clint Moore, Greg D. Rieves, Barry Slate, Donna K. Teal, Tazmen Carlisle, Amy Kirtley-Hill, Kristy Parton, Debbie Shoffner, Cathy Edwards Simrell, Lynette Dickerson, Mark Rainey

www.themailbox.com

©2004 The Mailbox® Books
All rights reserved.
ISBN10 #1-56234-561-3 • ISBN13 #978-156234-561-7

Printed in the United States
10 9 8 7 6 5 4

SEPTEMBER

School Bus

School Bus Spectacles

While students wear these neat school bus glasses, focus their attention on bus rules and routines.

Materials (per child)

glasses cutout (see Teacher Tips)
precut bus label (page 16)
two 12" lengths of yellow yarn
yellow tempera paint
black construction paper
hole puncher
paintbrush
scissors
glue

Directions

1. Paint the glasses cutout yellow and set it aside to dry.
2. Cut out two black construction paper wheels; then glue the wheels to the glasses.
3. Glue the bus label to the glasses.
4. Punch a hole in each top corner of the glasses. Tie a length of yarn onto each side.

Teacher Tips

● Copy a glasses pattern (page 16) onto tagboard for each child, cut it out, and then cut out the eyeholes with a craft knife.
● If desired, label each bus rider's glasses with the appropriate bus number.

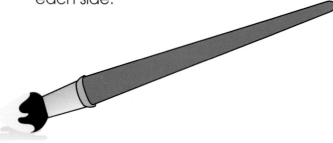

Amy Barsanti • Roper, NC

Collage Caddy

Youngsters will proudly place their school supplies in these portable, personalized caddies.

Materials (per child)

- plastic frosting container
- magazines, photos, and stickers
- plain white adhesive label
- clear Con-Tact covering
- scissors
- glue

Directions

1. Cut out magazine pictures or photos of favorite foods, activities, animals, or other items to reflect your personality. Or select stickers to represent some of these things.
2. Glue the cutouts and affix the stickers onto the container in collage fashion.
3. Create a name label and affix it to the container.
4. Cover the container with Con-Tact covering.
5. Fill the collage caddy with school supplies.

Teacher Tips

- To cover the container with ease, use a 3½" x 11" piece of Con-Tact covering.
- Each container holds 24 crayons, a pair of scissors, a small bottle of glue, and several pencils.

Margaret Southard • Cleveland, NY

Grandparents' Goodies Jar

Loving thoughts and wishes come with these goody jars filled with kisses! Invite youngsters to present these treat-filled jars to honor their grandparents (or special elderly friends) on National Grandparents Day.

Materials (per child)

- copy of rhyme circle (page 16)
- lidded small plastic container
- rubber band
- 4½" tissue paper circle
- small pieces of tissue paper in various colors
- diluted glue
- glue
- paintbrush
- scissors
- Hershey's Hugs candies
- Hershey's Kisses candies

Directions

1. Remove the jar lid; then paint a coat of diluted glue on the outside of the container.
2. Press tissue paper pieces onto the glue, overlapping them to cover the whole container
3. Paint another coat of diluted glue over the tissue paper. Allow the glue to dry.
4. Cut out the rhyme circle. Write the child's dictation of his grandparent's name on the cutout; then glue it onto the center of the tissue paper circle.
5. Put a few pieces of each candy into the container. Replace the lid; then cover the lid with the tissue paper circle, securing it with the rubber band.

Teacher Tips

- Dilute the glue with water until it is thin enough to be easily brushed onto the container.
- Invert the container before coating it with glue. This makes it easy for the child to cover the sides and bottom with tissue paper. Leave the container inverted to dry.

Susan DeRiso • Barrington, RI

"Photo-magnetic" Friends

When youngsters use these magnets to display their school work, they'll have a little help from their friends! And each family will gladly welcome the photo introduction of classmates provided by this unique idea.

Materials (per child)

- reprint of class photo
- craft sticks
- glue
- two 3" strips of magnetic tape

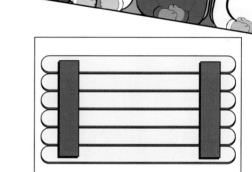

Directions

1. Glue craft sticks side by side on the back of the photo; then allow the glue to dry.
2. Attach a magnetic tape strip along each side of the photo backing as shown.

Teacher Tips

- Take several photos of the class; then choose your favorite photo and have a class quantity of reprints made.
- To help students and families match the names and faces of classmates, send home a list of student names corresponding to the photo.

Betty Silkunas • North Wales, PA

Good Neighbor Garland

Invite each child to decorate a house on one of these gorgeous garlands. Then border a class display about houses or neighborhoods with the finished products.

Materials (per garland)

- tagboard house tracer (see Teacher Tips)
- 6" x 24" newsprint strip
- scissors
- pencil
- markers

Directions

1. Using the width of the house tracer as a guide, accordion-fold the newsprint strip to create five sections.
2. Align the house with the bottom edge of the folded strip and then trace the roof, window, and door with a pencil.
3. Cut along the roof line and cut out the window and door openings through all thicknesses. Do not cut the sides of the house!
4. Carefully unfold the strip of houses. Then invite a different child to use markers to decorate each house on the resulting garland.
5. Write each child's dictated address on her house. If desired, back the window opening with a small photo of the child.

Teacher Tips
- To make a tracer, cut out a tagboard copy of the house pattern on page 17; then cut out the window and door openings.
- Cut a sheet of 18" x 24" newsprint into three 6" x 24" strips. Each strip of paper will make a five-house garland.

Carol Ann Bloom • State College, PA

Birthday Pop-Up Pal

Youngsters will pop out in grins and giggles when you greet each birthday child with this "bear-y" cute desk topper on his special day.

HAVE A "BEAR-Y" HAPPY BIRTHDAY!

Materials

- tagboard bear tracer (page 17)
- white 9" paper plate
- yellow tempera paint
- brown tempera paint
- paintbrush
- black marker
- craft knife
- tape

Directions

1. Turn the paper plate facedown; then paint the center brown and the outer rim yellow.
2. After the paint dries, label the outer rim with a birthday greeting.
3. Turn the plate over and fit the bear tracer to the inside curve of the plate rim. Trace the bear onto the plate as shown.
4. Use a craft knife to cut along the traced lines; then cut along the inner rim of the plate, as shown. (Do not cut this piece completely out.)
5. Add facial features to the pop-up bear on the painted side.
6. Carefully separate the cutout sections of the plate. Fold the bear and outer rim forward and the bear silhouette back so that the bear stands upright under the yellow arch.
7. Tape the pop-up pal desk topper to the child's desk as shown.

HAVE A "BEAR-Y" HAPPY BIRTHDAY!

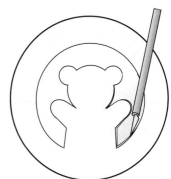

Teacher Tips

- If desired, make a keepsake pop-up pal for each child. To personalize the desk-topper, write the child's name on the bottom section of the plate rim.

Susan DeRiso • Barrington, RI

Starry Apple Surprise

Impress your little ones with a surprising apple fact—there's a star inside every apple! Then invite each child to create this happy apple reminder to share with his family.

In every apple near and far
Is a happy little star!

Materials (per child)

- copy of apple rhyme (page 19)
- 2 red construction paper copies of apple pattern (page 18)
- reduced white copy of apple pattern (see Teacher Tips)
- 12" length of red yarn
- green construction paper
- brown construction paper
- apple half (cut horizontally to reveal the star shape)
- red tempera paint
- paintbrush
- scissors
- glue
- hole puncher

Directions

1. Cut out the apple rhyme and all the apple patterns.
2. Cut out a brown stem and a green leaf from construction paper.
3. Glue the stem, leaf, and apple rhyme onto one red apple cutout.
4. Glue the reduced white apple cutout onto the other red apple cutout.
5. Paint the flat side of the apple half red; then make a print on the white apple cutout.
6. After the paint dries, stack the red apple cutouts so that the poem is on top, punch two holes at the top, and bind the cutouts together with yarn.

Teacher Tips

- Reduce the apple pattern (page 18) onto white paper to create the smaller "inside" pattern.
- Remove the seeds from the apple before making the apple print.

Susan DeRiso • Barrington, RI

Cool Apple Coaster

Use these cool coasters during your fall festivities or at snacktimes during your apple unit. Simply include a coaster with each child's table setting; then have her place her cool drink on the coaster.

Materials (per child)

- clear plastic yogurt lid
- green construction paper
- red yarn
- glue
- scissors

Directions

1. Squeeze a shallow pool of glue into the lid.
2. Press the yarn into the glue to create a spiral pattern.
3. Cut out green leaves and a stem; then glue the cutouts onto the apple. Allow the glue to dry.
4. To use, turn the coaster upside down (yarn side down) and set a drink on the coaster.

Teacher Tips

- Use a cotton ball dipped in rubbing alcohol to remove the date on the yogurt lid.
- Laminate the green paper for durability. This also makes it easy for children to cut out shapes from the paper.
- Use these coasters for cold drinks only!
- If desired, attach magnetic tape to each apple to create a decorative magnet.

Deborah Garmon • Groton, CT

Paper Plate Piggy

These cute critters make the perfect addition to your unit on farm animals. Display the piggies on a farm scene bulletin board or send them home with youngsters to share with their families.

Materials (per child)

- large paper plate
- small paper plate
- pink construction paper copy of pig patterns (page 19)
- one-half of a pink pipe cleaner
- pink tempera paint
- black tempera paint
- paintbrush
- pencil
- scissors
- glue
- tape

Directions

1. Paint the back of the large plate pink. Also paint the front of the small plate pink.
2. After the paint dries, glue the small plate onto the large plate to make a pig body.
3. Cut out the nose, ears, and feet patterns. Glue each cutout onto the pig as shown.
4. Use the black paint to make thumbprint eyes, nostrils, and hooves on the pig.
5. To create a tail, twist the pipe cleaner around a pencil and then slide it off. Tape the tail to the back of the pig.

Susan DeRiso • Barrington, RI

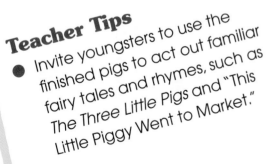

Teacher Tips
- Invite youngsters to use the finished pigs to act out familiar fairy tales and rhymes, such as *The Three Little Pigs* and "This Little Piggy Went to Market."

Molly Moo

Bag these "moo-velous" barn friends for your farm animals unit. Youngsters will enjoy using their bagged bovines in dramatic play or seeing them on a special display.

Materials (per child)

- white paper lunch bag
- white construction paper copy of cow patterns (page 20)
- black construction paper
- newspaper
- scissors
- glue
- stapler

Directions

1. Stuff the bag with crumpled pieces of newspaper; then staple the top closed.
2. Cut out the head and hoof patterns. Then cut out several cow spots and a tail from the black construction paper.
3. Glue the head, hooves, spots, and tail onto the bag as shown.

Teacher Tips

- Make a few snips in one end of each cow tail to fringe it.

Susan Bunyan • Dodge City, KS

Glasses and Bus Label Patterns
Use with "School Bus Spectacles" on page 6.

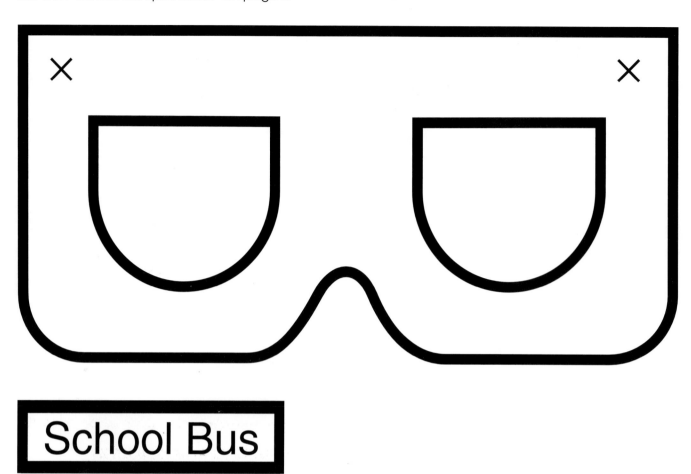

School Bus

Rhyme Circle
Use with "Grandparents' Goodies Jar" on page 8.

Bear Pattern
Use with "Birthday Pop-Up Pal" on page 11.

House Pattern
Use with "Good Neighbor Garland" on page 10.

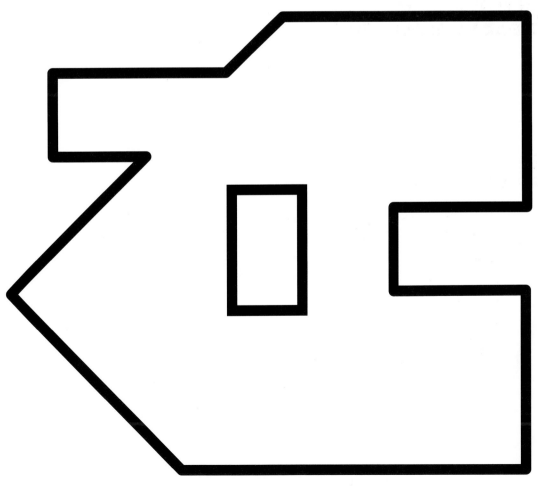

Apple Pattern
Use with "Starry Apple Surprise" on page 12.

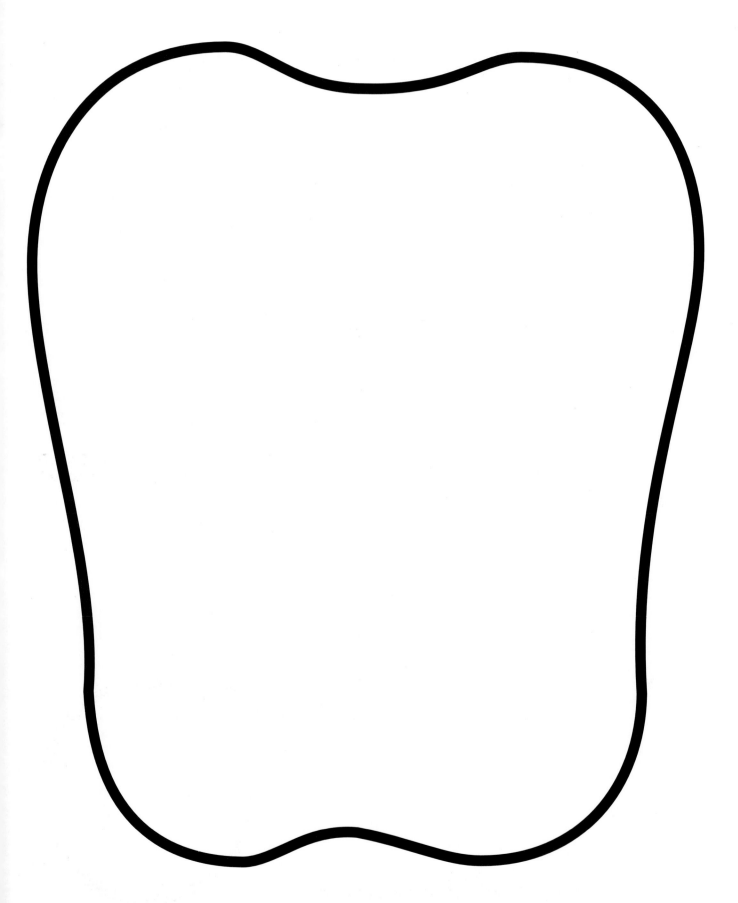

In every apple near and far
Is a happy little star!

Pig Patterns
Use with "Paper Plate Piggy" on page 14.

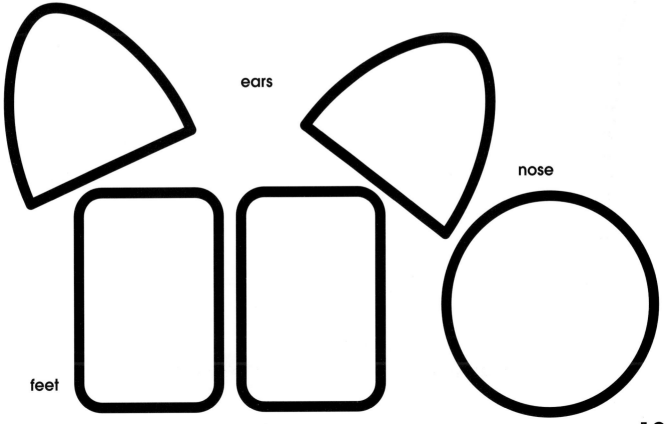

ears

nose

feet

Cow Patterns
Use with "Molly Moo" on page 15.

OCTOBER

Tube Tree

Bring the colors of fall to life with these beautiful stand-up trees. Invite youngsters to use their trees in their fall dramatic-play themes and then take them home to use as table decorations.

Materials (per child)

- toilet paper tube
- 3 plastic drinking straws
- 2" squares of red, yellow, and orange tissue paper
- 6" green construction paper square
- brown tempera paint
- paintbrush
- scissors
- glue
- hole puncher

Directions

1. Paint the tube and straws brown; then set them aside to dry.
2. After the paint dries, cut each straw into two or three lengths.
3. Beginning about one inch from one end of each straw, glue crinkled tissue paper squares along the length of the straw to create a leafy tree branch.
4. Punch a hole near the tube top for each straw branch; then insert each branch into a different hole.
5. Glue the upright tree onto the green paper square. Glue a few tissue paper leaves onto the green base to resemble fallen leaves.

Teacher Tips

- Pour glue into a foam plate; then use cotton swabs to apply the glue.
- Add a small amount of dishwashing liquid to the paint. This will prevent it from peeling off the straws.
- To secure the tree to the floor or table, attach small pieces of clay to the bottom of the base.

Bette Munda—Athens, GA

Tricolor Tree

Welcome the bright colors of fall into your classroom with these three-dimensional tree decorations.

Materials (per child)
- red, yellow, and orange tree cutouts (see Teacher Tips)
- scissors
- glue stick
- hole puncher
- length of yarn for hanging

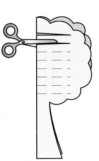

Directions
1. Fold each tree cutout in half vertically.
2. Cut slits in the leafy part of each tree where indicated.
3. Leaving each tree folded, use a glue stick to apply glue around the edges and on the trunk of each tree.
4. Press the trees together as shown.
5. After the glue dries, punch a hole in the treetop. Lace a yarn hanger through the hole.
6. Pull out every other slitted strip on each tree color to create a three-dimensional tree.

Teacher Tips
- To make a tree cutout, fold a sheet of construction paper in half vertically. Place the straight edge of the tree pattern (page 34) on the fold; then trace it and cut it out. Do not cut on the fold. (Each child will need three different colors of trees.)
- To retain the three-dimensional appearance of the completed tree, crease each slitted strip as you pull it out.

Susan Bunyan—Dodge City, KS

Clear Collage Leaf

Transform your classroom into an autumn wonderland with these creative leaf collages. Tape the finished projects to your windows, suspend them from the ceiling, or use them as display borders.

Materials (per child)

- leaf tracer (see Teacher Tips)
- two 8" squares of clear Con-Tact covering
- tissue paper in assorted fall colors
- permanent marker
- scissors

Directions

1. Cut tissue paper into very small pieces.
2. Peel the backing off one square of Con-Tact covering; then sprinkle tissue paper pieces onto it.
3. Peel the backing off the other Con-Tact square. Carefully press this square over the first one, sealing the tissue paper between them.
4. Trace the leaf pattern onto the square.
5. Cut out the leaf shape.

Teacher Tips

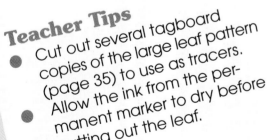

- Cut out several tagboard copies of the large leaf pattern (page 35) to use as tracers.
- Allow the ink from the permanent marker to dry before cutting out the leaf.

Patti Moeser—McFarland, WI

Leaf-Tailed Squirrel

Your little ones will fall for these unique bushy-tailed squirrels. Display these cute critters on a fall bulletin board to celebrate the season.

Materials (per child)

- squirrel pattern (see Teacher Tips)
- 2 white hole reinforcers
- small black pom-pom
- brown dried leaves
- glue
- scissors
- black marker

Directions

1. Cut out the squirrel pattern.
2. Glue leaves onto the squirrel tail.
3. Attach hole reinforcer eyes and then glue a pom-pom nose onto the squirrel's face.
4. Color inside the hole reinforcers.

Teacher Tips

- For each child, duplicate the squirrel pattern (page 36) onto brown or gray construction paper.
- Take your class on a nature walk to collect brown leaves.

Patti Moeser—McFarland, WI

Bouncy Spider

Put a little bounce into your spider studies with these cute creatures. Suspend the completed spiders from your classroom ceiling or send them home with your youngsters to share with their families.

Materials (per child)

tagboard tracers for spider, eyes, and mouth (see Teacher Tips)
black, red, and light green construction paper
length of yarn for hanging
crayons
scissors
glue
white pencil or crayon

Directions

1. Trace the spider twice on black paper. Then trace two eyes on green paper and a mouth on red paper. Cut out each piece.
2. Glue the mouth and eye cutouts onto one spider cutout.
3. Glue one end of the yarn to the back of the decorated spider.
4. Glue the two spider bodies together, leaving the legs free.
5. After the glue dries, fold the front legs forward and the back legs backward to give the spider a three-dimensional appearance.

Teacher Tips

- To make tracers, cut out tagboard copies of the spider, eye, and mouth patterns (page 37).
- Use a white pencil or crayon to trace the spider body on black construction paper.

Susan Bunyan—Dodge City, KS

Bat Hat

Your youngsters' imaginations will soar when they wear these bat hats in their dramatic-play activities.

Materials (per child)

- two 1½" x 12" black construction paper strips
- bat head and wing tracers (see Teacher Tips)
- black construction paper
- scissors
- glue
- colored chalk
- stapler

Directions

1. Use chalk to trace a bat head and two wings onto the black paper; then cut out the pieces.
2. Draw bat facial features on the head.
3. Staple the paper strips together to create a fitted headband.
4. Glue the head onto the headband.
5. Staple the wing cutouts to the headband; then fold them out as shown.

Teacher Tips

- Copy and cut out several tagboard bat head and wing patterns (page 34) to use as tracers.
- Use one sheet of black construction paper (cut into six 1½-inch strips) to make headbands for every three children.
- To prevent the chalk from smearing, spray it lightly with hairspray.

Valerie Wood Smith—Morgantown, PA

Candy Corn Wreath

This sweet wreath makes the perfect seasonal decoration for a wall, door, or window. Encourage each child to take her wreath home to display in a prominent place.

Directions

1. Paint the back of each paper-plate ring orange. Set the rings aside to dry.
2. Glue the candy corn onto the painted side of one paper-plate ring. Allow the glue to dry.
3. Glue the two rings together as shown, trapping the ends of a length of yarn between the plates to create a hanger.
4. Glue a ribbon bow onto the bottom of the wreath.

Teacher Tips

- For each child, cut out the center of two paper plates to create rings.
- Give each child a few extra pieces of candy corn to nibble on while she makes her wreath.

Deborah Garmon—Groton, CT

Pumpkin Parts

Teach students about the different parts of a pumpkin with this activity. Then encourage each child to share his pumpkin knowledge with his family.

Materials (per child)

- large and small pumpkin tracers (see Teacher Tips)
- orange, yellow, and green construction paper
- orange crinkle paper strips
- 10 paper pumpkin seed cutouts
- pencil
- scissors
- glue

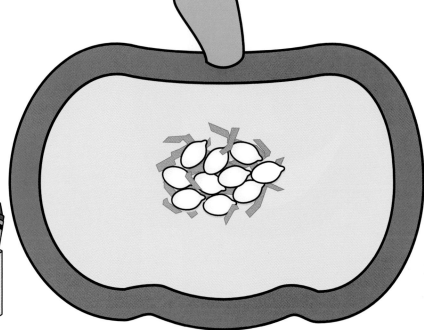

Directions

1. Trace the large pumpkin onto orange paper and the small pumpkin onto yellow paper. Cut out each shape.
2. Glue the yellow cutout onto the orange one to create a pumpkin with a thin outer skin and a thick inner flesh.
3. Cut out a green pumpkin stem; then glue it onto the pumpkin.
4. Glue the crinkle strips onto the pumpkin center to represent stringy pulp fibers.
5. Glue the seeds on and around the crinkle-strip pumpkin fibers.

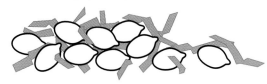

Teacher Tips
- In advance, cut out 10 white construction paper pumpkin seeds for each child.
- Cut out tagboard copies of the large and small pumpkin patterns (page 38) to use as tracers.

Bonnie Cave—Duluth, GA

Happy Jack Magnet

Spread some seasonal cheer with these smiling jack-o'-lantern magnets. Invite each youngster to take his happy jack home to display on a magnetic surface.

Materials (per child)

- juice can lid
- orange glue (see Teacher Tips)
- magnetic tape
- green construction paper
- scissors
- black permanent marker

magnetic tape

Directions

1. Fill the juice can lid with orange glue to create a pumpkin.
2. Cut a pumpkin stem out of the green paper and place it on the juice can pumpkin.
3. Set the pumpkin aside to dry (for about two days).
4. When the glue is completely dry, gently pop the pumpkin out of the lid.
5. Draw a happy face on the pumpkin with the permanent marker.
6. Attach a piece of magnetic tape to the back of the pumpkin as shown.

Teacher Tips
- Mix equal amounts of red and yellow food coloring with white glue to make orange glue.
- Before sending the magnets home with students, use them in your math center with a magnetboard to reinforce counting skills.

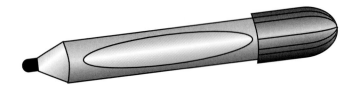

adapted from an idea by Patti Moeser—McFarland, WI

Jack Sack

These adorable, easy-to-make jack sacks do double duty as seasonal decorations and party bags! Display the bags in the classroom; then send them home with students on the day of your celebration.

Materials (per child)

- small paper bag
- orange tempera paint
- small sponge
- black construction paper
- scissors
- glue
- yarn
- hole puncher
- age-appropriate party treats

Directions

1. Sponge-paint the bag orange and then allow it to dry.
2. Cut out jack-o'-lantern facial features from black paper.
3. Glue the facial features onto the bag.
4. Put the party treats in the bag; then fold the top down.
5. Punch two holes in the folded bag top. Lace a length of yarn through the holes and tie it into a bow.

Teacher Tips

- Clip a clothespin onto each sponge to create a handle for it. This will help reduce the amount of paint that gets on your little ones' hands.
- To use the bags for decorations only, simply stuff each one with crumpled newspaper instead of treats.

Anita Edlund—Farragut, TN

Candy Corn Bucket

Use these cute projects as treat holders for a Halloween or fall party! Line each finished cup with orange or black tissue paper and then fill it with candy corn.

Materials (per child)

- small polystyrene cup
- orange or black pipe cleaner
- orange glue paint (see Teacher Tips)
- yellow glue paint
- paintbrush
- black permanent marker

Directions

1. Paint a yellow strip around the middle of the polystyrene cup.
2. Paint an orange strip around the top of the cup, so the cup resembles a piece of candy corn.
3. After the paint dries, use a permanent marker to draw a face on the cup.
4. Poke one end of a pipe cleaner through each side of the cup rim and twist the pipe cleaner ends in place to make a handle.

Teacher Tips

- Make glue paint by mixing two parts white glue with one part tempera paint.
- Use a pushpin to make holes in the cup rims. This will make it easy for the children to poke the pipe-cleaner ends into the cup.

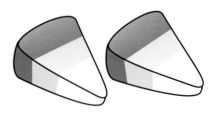

Linda Ludlow—Pittsboro, IN

Boo! Mask

Delight youngsters with this simple mask that communicates a seasonally contagious message. Boo!

Materials (per child)

- 3" to 4" black die-cut letters to spell *BOO*
- two 1½" x 12" strips of orange construction paper
- glue
- stapler

Directions

1. Glue the two orange strips together to make one long strip.
2. Glue the two *O*s along the lower edge of the orange strip to create eyeholes.
3. Glue the *B* above the eyeholes.
4. After the glue dries, staple the ends of the strip together to create a fitted mask.

Teacher Tips

- Precut each 9" x 12" sheet of orange construction paper into six 1½-inch-wide strips. Three masks can be made from each sheet of paper.
- Overlap the *O*s as necessary so that the child can see through them.

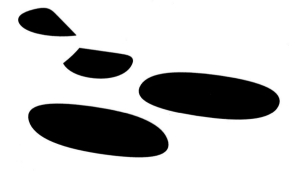

Carol Ann Bloom—State College, PA

Tree Pattern
Use with "Tricolor Tree" on page 23.

Bat Patterns
Use with "Bat Hat" on page 27.

head

wing

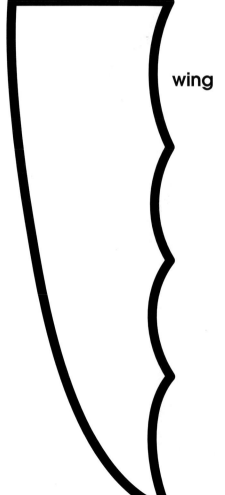

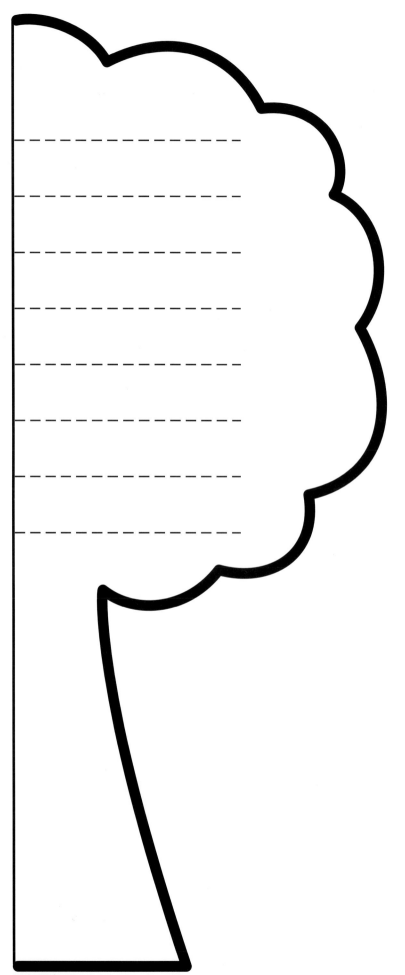

Squirrel Pattern
Use with "Leaf-Tailed Squirrel" on page 25.

spider

eyes

mouth

Pumpkin Parts Patterns

Use with "Pumpkin Parts" on page 29.

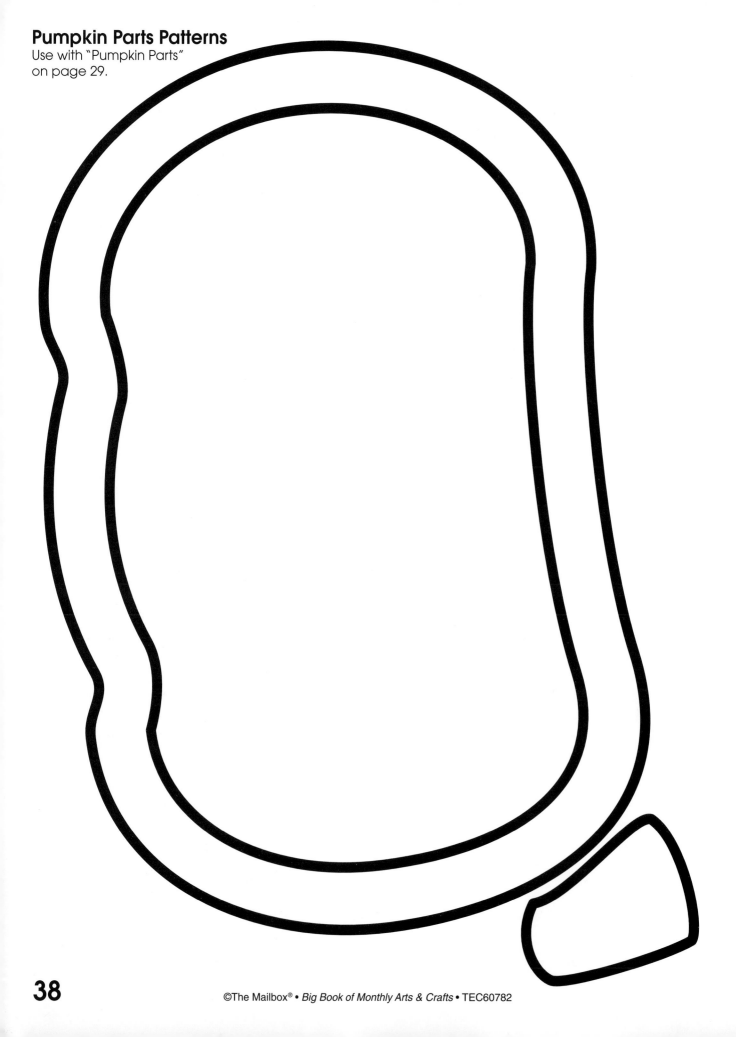

NOVEMBER

Turkey Topper

Top off your students' Thanksgiving fun with these floppy turkey headbands.

Materials (per child)

- yellow construction paper turkey body (page 53)
- red construction paper turkey wattle (page 53)
- orange construction paper turkey beak (page 53)
- 12" x 36" length of brown bulletin board paper
- 2 tiny black pom-poms
- scissors
- glue
- pencil
- stapler

Directions

1. Cut out all the turkey patterns. Glue the wattle and beak onto the body. Attach the pom-pom eyes above the beak.
2. Cut a three-inch-wide strip off one end of the brown paper to make a wing strip. Trim the length and the corners of the wing strip; then fringe-cut each end.
3. Glue the wing strip to the back of the turkey body.
4. To make the headband, fold the long brown paper into thirds; then make three equidistant cuts through all thicknesses as shown.
5. Round the corners of each section to create turkey tail feathers.
6. Glue the turkey body onto the headband.
7. Overlap the ends of the headband; then staple them together, sized to fit.

Teacher Tip

- If desired, wrap the fringed wing ends around a pencil and then release them to give the wings a feathery look. Curl the tail feathers in the same manner.

Susan Bunyan—Dodge City, KS

Sparkly Cornucopia

This cornucopia is a sparkling reminder of giving thanks. Display the cornucopias on a bulletin board for your students and class visitors to enjoy.

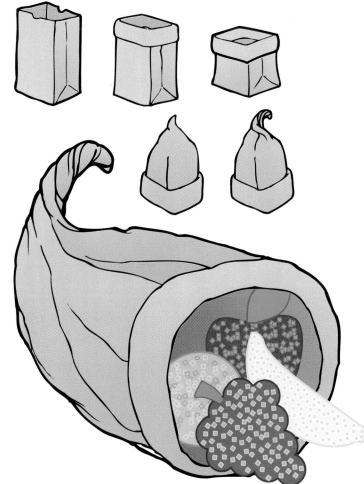

Materials (per child)

- copy of each fruit pattern (see Teacher Tips)
- brown paper lunch bag
- gold, red, purple, and orange glitter
- green construction paper
- glue
- paintbrush
- scissors

Directions

1. Cut out each fruit pattern.
2. Paint a fruit cutout with glue; then sprinkle it with the corresponding color of glitter. Repeat the process with each fruit.
3. Cut out a green stem or leaf (if appropriate) for each fruit. Glue the cutouts onto the fruit.
4. Fold the top of the bag down about one inch; then fold it down again.
5. Pull the bottom of the bag out, and then twist it to form a cornucopia as shown.
6. Glue the glittery fruit cutouts in the opening of the cornucopia.

Teacher Tips

- For each child, make a copy of each fruit pattern (page 54) as follows: a red apple, a yellow banana, an orange orange, and purple grapes.
- As an alternative (to cut back on glitter), mix each color of glitter into a different batch of white glue. Thin each mixture with water. Then paint each cutout with the corresponding color of glitter glue.

Kimberli Carrier—Nashua, NH

Turkey Candy Dish

Use this handy candy dish during your class Thanksgiving celebration. Afterward, invite each child to take her dish home to refill with a holiday treat for a special family member.

Materials (per child)

- tagboard
- construction paper in various colors (including brown)
- tiny black pom-pom
- nut cup
- pencil
- scissors
- glue
- holiday treat (such as candy corn or cereal mix)

Directions

1. Trace your hand on the tagboard. Cut out the hand outline.
2. Tear an assortment of construction paper (including the brown) into small pieces.
3. Glue the brown pieces onto the palm and thumb of the hand cutout to resemble the turkey body.
4. Glue the other colors onto each finger to resemble turkey feathers.
5. Cut out a red wattle and orange beak. Glue these onto the turkey head. Attach the pom-pom (eye).
6. Glue a nut cup onto the turkey body.
7. After the glue dries, fill the cup with a holiday treat.

Teacher Tips

- To encourage youngsters to tear the paper into small pieces, use construction paper scraps and strips.
- Pair students; then have each child trace her partner's hand. Help each child, as necessary, cut out her own hand outline.

Kathy Brand—Greenwood Lake, NY

Thankful Thoughts Picture Frame

Invite each child to highlight his illustrated thoughts of thankfulness with this unique picture frame. Then display all the pictures in art-gallery fashion. Periodically change the art in the frames to allow students to show off the many things for which they are thankful.

Materials (per child)

- picture frame front and back (see Teacher Tip)
- craft glue
- 4" x 6" plain index card
- crayons
- tagboard strip

Directions

1. Color the picture frame front.
2. Glue the frame front to the back along only the outer edges of three sides; then allow the glue to dry.
3. Illustrate the index card with a thankful thought.
4. Insert the picture into the open edge of the frame; then label a strip of tagboard with the artist's name. Display the art and name label together.

Teacher Tip

- For each child, copy the frame pattern (page 55) twice onto tagboard. Cut out both frames; then cut out the center of just one frame to use as the frame front.

Native American Shaker

Add to your Thanksgiving celebration with this Native American shaker. Invite youngsters to dance and shake their shakers as you play a rhythmic drum pattern.

Materials (per child)

- lidded plastic soda bottle (20 oz.) with bottom removed (see Teacher Tips)
- two 8" tissue paper squares in different colors
- permanent markers in assorted colors
- 2 tbsp. unpopped popcorn
- scissors
- hot glue
- stapler
- wide clear tape

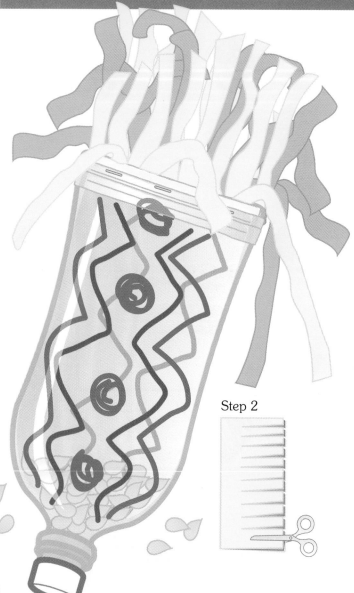

Step 2

Directions

1. Use permanent markers to decorate the bottle with a Native American design.
2. Stack the two tissue paper squares; then fold them in half. Fringe-cut the folded paper, leaving a 1 ½-inch border of uncut paper on the folded end.
3. Pour two tablespoons of popcorn into the bottle; then staple the bottom of the bottle closed, trapping the intact ends of the fringed tissue paper inside.
4. To securely seal the contents of the shaker, wrap wide, clear tape around the stapled end of the bottle.

Teacher Tips

- In advance, cut off the bottom of the bottle. Cover the cut edges with tape to protect little hands. Then hot-glue the lid onto the bottle.
- Use a cotton swab dipped in alcohol to erase stray marks left by the markers.

adapted from an idea by Margaret Southard—Cleveland, NY

Shake 'n' Stamp Placemat

What's shakin'? It's the fun foil shape stamps used to create this multisensory placemat! Laminate each child's placemat, and then send it home for her to use during her family's Thanksgiving meal.

Materials (per child)

- 2 sheets of 9" x 12" white construction paper
- 8" length of foil
- ¼ cup uncooked rice
- shallow trays of tempera paint colors
- paintbrushes
- glue
- scissors

Directions

1. To make a shape stamp, put the rice in the center of the foil. Fold the foil as shown; then twist the ends together to create a handle. Gently mold the foil-covered rice into the desired shape, and then flatten the bottom of the stamper.
2. Use the shape stamp and the paint color of your choice to decorate one sheet of paper. Allow the paint to dry.
3. Fold the second sheet of paper in half lengthwise, and then unfold it.
4. Use a paintbrush to paint a simple design on one side of the paper; then fold the paper over the paint to create a mirror image of the design.
5. After the paint dries, cut the folded paper in half along the fold.
6. Glue each half onto the ends of the first paper to make a placemat.

Teacher Tips

- Group youngsters into pairs; then invite the partners to share their shape stamps with each other.
- To avoid creating paint pools on the placemat, dip each stamp into the paint, wipe off the excess paint on the tray rim, and then stamp the paper.

Indian Corn

Harvest a crop of this colorful corn to create a seasonal bulletin board. Use the display to inspire youngsters to brainstorm a list of foods made from corn. Then serve your class a popcorn snack.

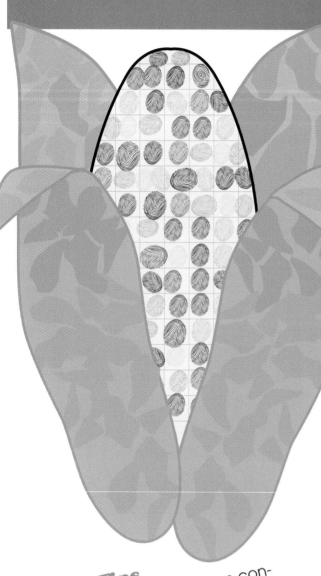

Materials (per child)

- manila corncob (pattern on page 56)
- corn husk tracer (see Teacher Tips)
- large brown paper bag
- red, yellow, orange, and brown stamp pads
- scissors
- glue

Directions

1. Cut out the corncob pattern.
2. Using a different finger for each stamp pad color, fill the squares on the cob cutout with fingerprints.
3. Trace the corn husk four times onto the unprinted side of the bag; then cut out each outline.
4. Crumple each husk cutout, and then smooth it out.
5. Glue two husks to the back of the corn and two to the front as shown. Fold the front husks forward to create a three-dimensional effect.

Teacher Tips

- If desired, substitute brown construction paper or bulletin board paper for the husks.
- To make a husk tracer, cut out a tagboard copy of the husk pattern on page 56.
- As an alternative to colored stamp pads, use colored pencils to color the grid on the corn.

Susan Bunyan—Dodge City, KS

Twinkling Traffic Light

Enhance your students' dramatic-play activities and their knowledge of traffic rules with this traffic light project.

Materials (per child)

- half sheet of yellow construction paper (cut lengthwise)
- piece of 4½" x 12" tagboard
- red, yellow, and green colored corn-syrup paint (see Teacher Tip)
- red, gold, and green glitter (optional)
- 3½" circle tracer (such as a plastic lid)
- pencil
- paintbrush
- hole puncher
- yarn
- scissors
- glue

Directions

1. Trace three circles (as shown) onto the tagboard.
2. Using the corn-syrup paint, paint the middle circle yellow, the bottom circle green, and the top one red. If desired, sprinkle a corresponding color of glitter on each circle. (Allow approximately three days for drying time.)
3. Trace three circles onto the yellow paper and cut them out. Glue the remaining yellow piece onto the painted tagboard as shown.
4. Punch a hole above the red circle.
5. Attach a yarn hanger to the top of the traffic light.

Step 1

Step 2

Step 3

Teacher Tip

- To make corn-syrup paint, stir food coloring into clear corn syrup until the desired color is achieved.

Patti Moeser—McFarland, WI

Beautiful Bookmark

What makes this bookmark so beautiful? The uniquely personal statement that it makes about its creator! Encourage youngsters to use their personalized bookmarks at school during Children's Book Week (in November) and then later at home.

Materials (per child)

- tagboard strip (to serve as the bookmark)
- small school photo of child
- supply of magazines and catalogs
- construction paper scraps
- clear Con-Tact covering
- ribbon
- scissors
- glue
- hole puncher
- black marker

Directions

1. Cut a designer edge around the photo; then glue it onto the bookmark.
2. Cut out magazine and catalog pictures representing your favorite things. Glue them onto the bookmark.
3. Cut a shape out of colorful construction paper. Label the shape with your name and then glue it onto the bookmark.
4. Cover the front of the bookmark with clear Con-Tact covering.
5. Write the title of a favorite book on the back of the bookmark.
6. Punch three holes along the bottom of the bookmark; then tie three lengths of ribbon to it.

Teacher Tips

- In advance, label each piece of tagboard with "My favorite book is…"
- If desired, invite students to bring in personal photos to use on their bookmarks.

Susan DeRiso—Barrington, RI

Shooting Star

Send youngsters' imaginations into outer space with this shimmering shooting star. Hang these stars from your ceiling; then invite each child to describe an imaginary ride on a shooting star.

Materials (per child)

- 2 yellow construction paper stars (page 57)
- 2 gold sparkle pipe cleaners
- tissue paper
- gold glitter
- scissors
- water-thinned glue
- paintbrush
- hole puncher
- nylon thread

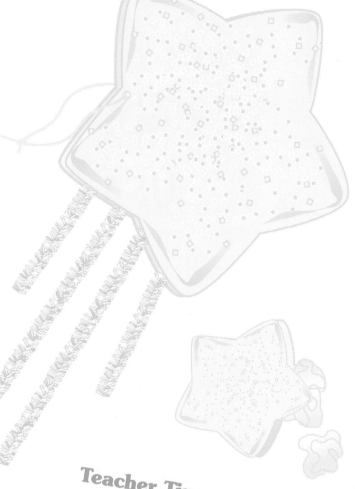

Directions

1. Cut out each star.
2. Paint each star cutout with water-thinned glue. Sprinkle glitter onto the glue; then set the stars aside to dry.
3. Cut one pipe cleaner into two different lengths. Cut the other pipe cleaner in half.
4. Glue the stars together along the back edges, leaving an opening between two points of the star.
5. After the glue dries, stuff crumpled tissue paper into the opening.
6. Insert the pipe cleaners between the two stars (as shown) to create the shooting star "streaks." Then glue the open edges together.
7. Punch a hole in the star; then tie a nylon hanger onto the star.

Teacher Tips
- Enlarge the star patterns on page 57 as desired.
- Have the child decide whether her star will shoot up, down, or across the sky; then punch the hole in the star so that it hangs as she desires.

Margaret Southard—Cleveland, NY

Super Spaceship

Step 1

Step 2

Step 3

Step 4

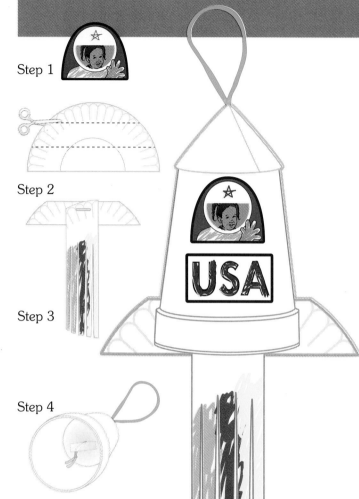

Enhance your space unit with these personalized spaceships. Three, two, one...blastoff!

Directions

1. Cut out the spaceship patterns. Color all the patterns; then cut out the opening in the helmet. Back the opening with the photo.
2. Cut two 1 ½-inch-wide strips from the straight edge of the plate half. Color one strip to resemble flames; then cut several long slits in the strip.
3. Staple the strip of flames onto the second strip (the wing strip) as shown.
4. Invert the cup and poke a hole in the bottom. Then poke both ends of a length of yarn through the hole and knot it to make a hanger for the spaceship (cup). Tape the knot to the inside of the cup.
5. Wrap the dome cutout around the yarn hanger to create the top of the spaceship. Glue the ends together; then glue the dome in place onto the spaceship.
6. Glue the window and label cutouts onto the spaceship.
7. Cut a 1¼-inch slit on opposite sides of the spaceship bottom; then insert the wings.

Susan DeRiso—Barrington, RI

Teacher Tips
- Use pushpins to hold the window cutout in place while the glue dries.
- If desired, copy each child's photo; then use the copy in the spaceship window.

50

Bear Cave

Shhh! Don't wake the hibernating bear! Use this activity to reinforce your unit on animal homes; then send each child home with his project to share the fun surprise with his family.

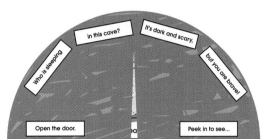

Materials (per child)

- bear and text patterns (page 58)
- paper plate
- brown tempera paint
- crayons
- paintbrush
- scissors
- glue

Directions

1. Paint the back of the paper plate brown.
2. After the paint dries, cut the plate in half. Starting at the middle of the straight edge, cut a long slit in one plate half (as shown).
3. Color and cut out the bear pattern; then cut out the text patterns.
4. Glue the bear cutout onto the front of the intact plate half. Glue the plate halves together (with the unpainted sides facing in).
5. Glue the text strips onto the front of the bear cave as shown.
6. After the glue dries, fold the front flaps up to reveal the surprise in the cave; then unfold them to hide the snoozing bear again.

Teacher Tip

- Use clothespins to hold the plates together while the glue dries.

Susan DeRiso—Barrington, RI

Migrating Geese

When winter comes,
Away they fly.
A flock of geese
Honk–honk "Good-bye!"

Wish our fine-feathered friends a safe flight as they migrate south for the winter. This unique activity is the perfect addition to your study of animals in the winter.

Materials (per child)

- geese text (page 58)
- paper plate
- sheet of blue construction paper
- brown tempera paint
- gray tempera paint
- white chalk
- scissors
- paintbrushes
- glue

Directions

1. Cut the plate (similar to the one shown above) to resemble a tree.
2. Paint the tree brown.
3. Cut several pairs of short strips from the rim scraps of the paper plates. Paint the strips gray.
4. When the paint is dry, glue the tree to the blue construction paper.
5. Arrange the short strips to resemble geese. Then glue the rim of each wing to the background.
6. Cut out the text and glue it onto the picture.
7. Use chalk to draw snow on the ground, on the tree, and in the sky.

Teacher Tips

- If gray paint is not available, mix white and black paint together.
- To keep the chalk from smearing, spray a light coat of hairspray over the completed picture.

adapted from an idea by Susan DeRiso—Barrington, RI

wattle

body

beak

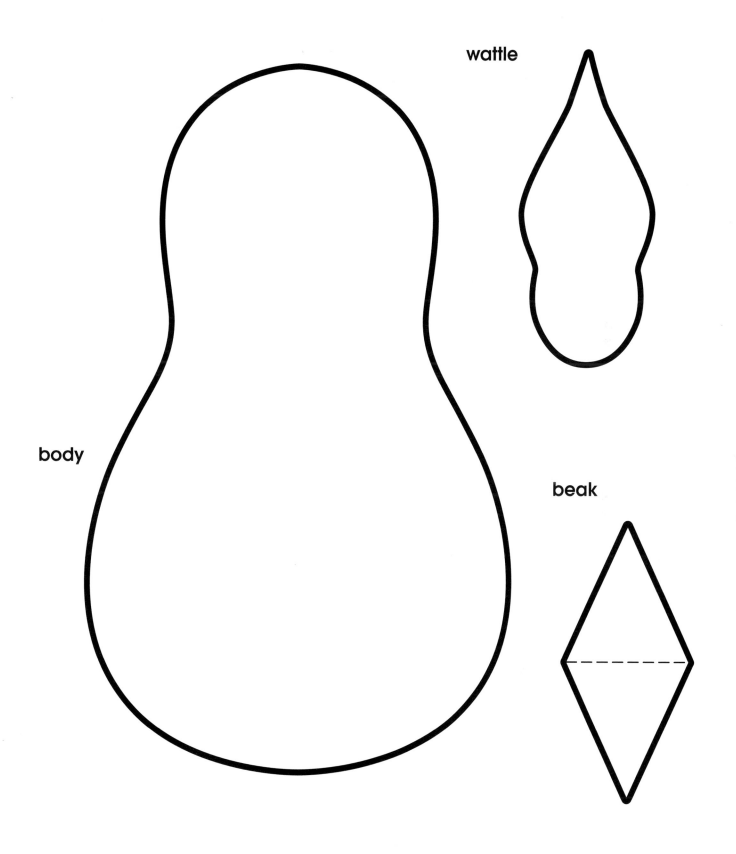

Fruit Patterns

Use with "Sparkly Cornucopia" on page 41.

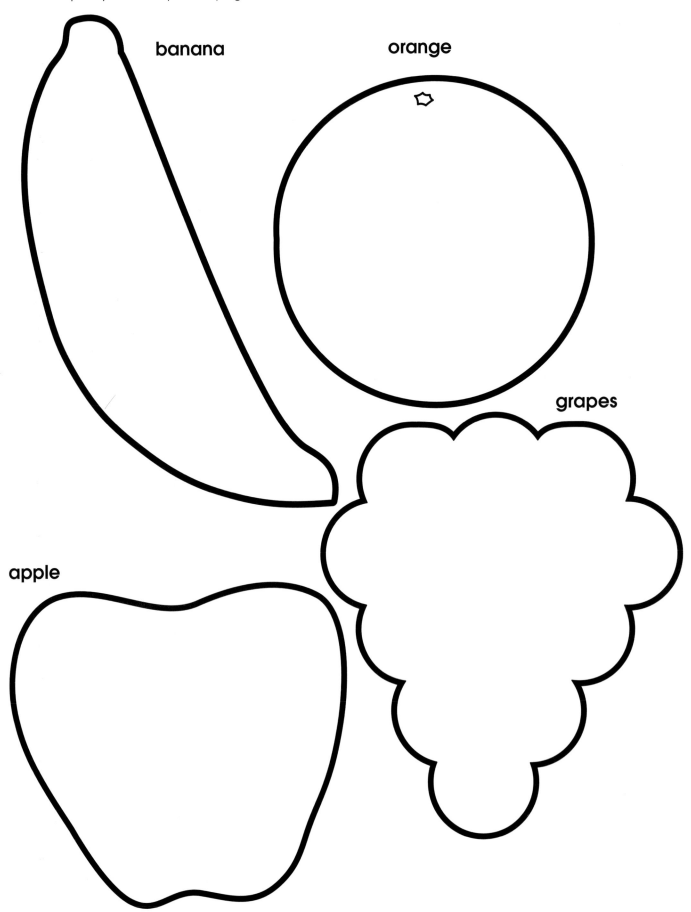

banana

orange

grapes

apple

Corn Patterns
Use with "Indian Corn" on page 46.

corn

husk

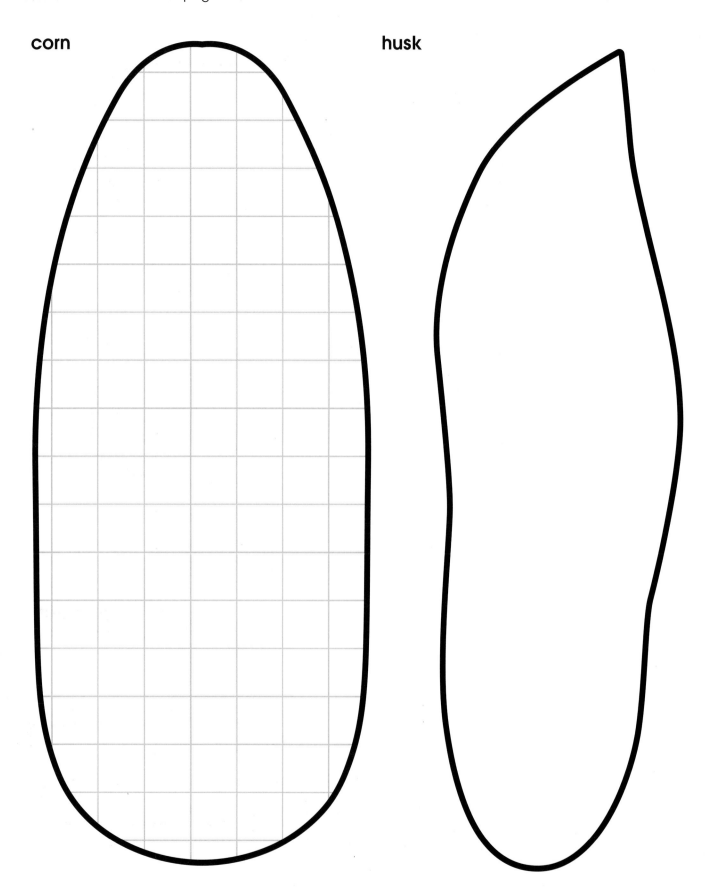

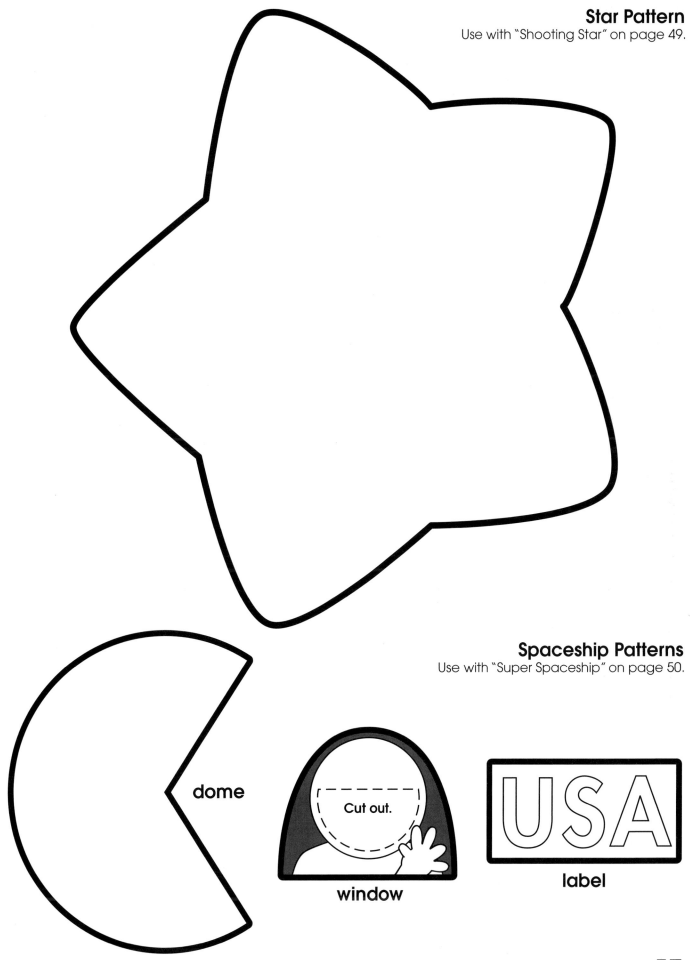

Star Pattern
Use with "Shooting Star" on page 49.

Spaceship Patterns
Use with "Super Spaceship" on page 50.

dome

Cut out.

window

USA

label

Bear and Text Patterns
Use with "Bear Cave" on page 51.

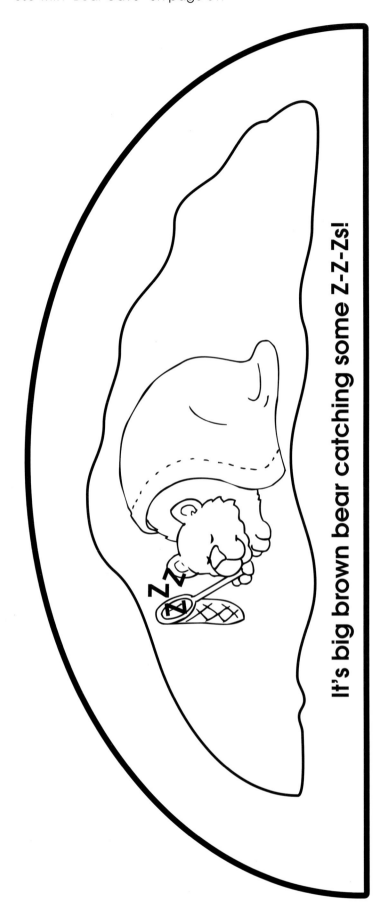

It's big brown bear catching some Z-Z-Zs!

Who is sleeping
in this cave?
It's dark and scary,
but you are brave!
Open the door.
Peek in to see...

Geese Text Pattern
Use with "Migrating Geese" on page 52.

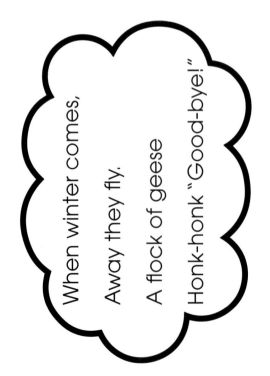

When winter comes,
Away they fly.
A flock of geese
Honk-honk "Good-bye!"

DECEMBER

"Hand-y" Holiday Ornament

This personalized ornament will be a hands-down favorite! When the projects are complete, have each child wrap his ornament as a holiday gift for a loved one.

Materials (per child)

- cornstarch dough (see Teacher Tip)
- knife (for adult use)
- cookie sheet
- oven
- small photo of child
- felt
- tiny sequins
- tempera paint
- paintbrushes
- scissors
- craft glue
- ribbon
- round film canister
- drinking straw
- clear acrylic

Directions

1. Press a portion of the dough to about ¼ inch thick. Have a child press his hand into the dough to make a handprint.
2. Cut out the handprint with a knife. Use the film canister to cut out a hole from the center of the hand. Use the straw to cut out a hole near the edge of the palm.
3. Bake the dough hands on an ungreased cookie sheet at 200° for three hours. Then set them aside for a day to harden completely.
4. Paint each hand, and then glue on colorful sequins as desired.
5. When the project is dry, spray the hand with a clear acrylic; then let it dry.
6. Glue the photo to the back of the hand so that it shows through the opening. Then back the photo with a piece of felt.
7. String a length of ribbon through the small hole and tie the ends together to create a hanger.

Julie A. Koczur

Teacher Tip
- Dough for eight ornaments: In a large pot, mix one cup each of cornstarch, salt, and water. Stir over low heat until the dough is the consistency of firm mashed potatoes. Let the dough cool, covering it with a damp cloth to prevent drying.

"Ginger-bag" House

This delightful decoration looks good enough to eat—but don't! It's a feast for the *eyes* only! After each child completes his "ginger-bag" house, secretly stuff a few holiday treats inside for a surprise at a later time.

Materials (per child)

- small brown paper bag
- 6" brown square (cut from a paper grocery bag)
- assorted colors of construction paper
- white paint pen (or white paint and a thin paintbrush)
- white ribbon
- scissors
- glue
- hole puncher
- newspaper

Directions

1. About halfway down, fold the top of the bag back.
2. Use the paint pen (or paintbrush) to paint a decorative edge around the sides and bottom of the front of the bag. Also paint an edge around the brown square (roof).
3. Cut out a white window and door; then glue each piece onto the house.
4. Cut out paper candy shapes and glue them onto the house.
5. After the paint and glue dry, unfold the paper bag and stuff it with newspaper. Then fold down just the top two inches of the bag.
6. Fold the roof in half; then place the fold on top of the bag (as shown).
7. Punch two holes through all thicknesses near the fold. Thread a length of ribbon through the holes and then tie a bow in the front.

Sue DeRiso—Barrington, RI

Folded roof goes over folded bag.

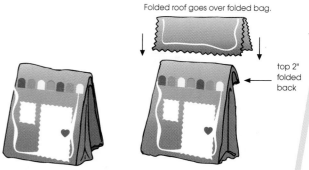

top 2" folded back

Teacher Tip
- If desired, use decorative scissors to cut out the roof, door, and window.

Gingerbread Friends

When each child creates this "scent-sational" string of gingerbread friends, he can use it as a decorative garland or a pretty gift necklace for a special loved one. (Note: These are not edible.)

Materials

- baking dough (see Teacher Tips)
- large bowl
- red and green food coloring
- ground cinnamon, ginger, and cloves
- gingerbread people cookie cutters
- rolling pin
- coffee stirrer
- cookie sheet
- oven
- white paint pen
- fine-tipped permanent markers
- small pom-poms
- craft glue
- thin ribbon

Directions

1. Mix into the dough about 20 drops each of red and green food coloring and one teaspoon each of cinnamon, ginger, and cloves.
2. Roll out a portion of the dough to about ¼ inch thick; then cut out three people shapes.
3. Place the cutouts on an ungreased cookie sheet. Use the coffee stirrer to poke a hole near the end of the arms of each dough person.
4. Bake the dough people at 200° for three hours; then allow them to air-dry for about three days. (If desired, eliminate the baking by air-drying the cutouts for about seven days.)
5. Decorate each gingerbread person with the paint pen, markers, and pom-poms.
6. Tie the gingerbread friends together with ribbon. Tie a longer ribbon to the two outside arms.

Margaret Southard—Cleveland, NY

Teacher Tips

- To make baking dough for 12 gingerbread people, mix together 2½ cups of flour, ½ cup of salt, and 1 cup of water. Add flour as needed to form a firm dough.
- If desired, paint the front of each gingerbread person with brown tempera paint. Allow the paint to dry before adding features to each shape.

Toy Soldier Mask

Enhance your students' dramatic-play activities with these fun toy soldier masks. Later, you might even invite them to march with their masks in a game of Follow-the-Leader.

Materials (per child)

- tagboard mask tracers (see Teacher Tips)
- 9" paper plate
- black, red, yellow, and blue construction paper
- 6" length of yellow ribbon
- wide craft stick
- regular craft stick (optional)
- chalk
- scissors
- craft glue
- black marker or crayon
- clothespins
- stapler

Directions

1. Fold the plate in half; then cut out an eye opening in the top third of the plate as shown.
2. Use chalk to trace the hat onto black paper; then cut it out.
3. Trace the circle two times onto both red and yellow paper; then cut out all four circles.
4. Trace and cut out several feathers in the desired colors: red, yellow, or blue.
5. Glue the ribbon, yellow circles, and feathers onto the hat as shown.
6. Glue red circle cheeks onto the inside of the paper plate; then draw on a mouth and nose.
7. Squeeze a line of glue along the plate rim above the eyehole; then attach the hat to the mask. Use clothespins to hold the hat in place while the glue dries.
8. Glue a wide craft stick handle to the mask.

Sue DeRiso—Barrington, RI

Teacher Tips

- To make tracers, trace each mask pattern (page 73) onto tagboard; then cut it out.
- If desired, use craft feathers instead of paper feathers on the hat.
- If the hat does not stand up, reinforce it by sliding a regular craft stick between the plate rim and the hat. Then glue it in place.

Candle Pencil Topper

Brighten up each child's writing skills with this versatile pencil topper. Then invite youngsters to convert their toppers into finger puppets to use with their favorite candle songs and rhymes.

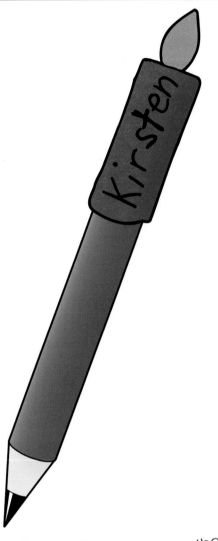

Materials (per child)

- 3" felt square
- orange felt
- fabric marker
- craft glue
- pencil
- scissors

Directions

1. Cut out an orange felt flame.
2. Draw a glue line along three edges of the felt square. Fold the square in half, inserting the flame into the glued top of the resulting candle.
3. After the glue dries, write your name (or initials) on the candle.
4. To use as a pencil topper, simply slide a pencil into the opening at the bottom of the candle.

Teacher Tip
- If desired, add sparkle to the candle by gluing gold glitter onto the felt flame.

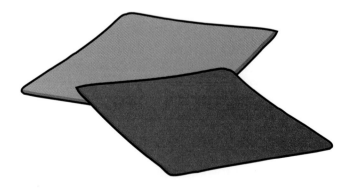

Sue DeRiso—Barrington, RI

Paper Plate Menorah

Make this special menorah to reinforce the candle-lighting ceremony followed during the eight-day Hanukkah celebration.

Materials (per child)

- tagboard menorah tracer (see Teacher Tips)
- white text box (pattern on page 74)
- blue construction paper candles (pattern on page 74)
- 9" paper plate
- orange construction paper
- yellow tempera paint
- scissors
- paintbrush
- glue

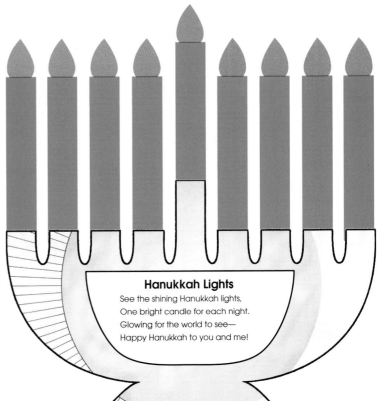

Hanukkah Lights
See the shining Hanukkah lights,
One bright candle for each night.
Glowing for the world to see—
Happy Hanukkah to you and me!

Directions

1. Trace the tagboard menorah onto the paper plate, fitting it to the curve of the plate. Then cut out the resulting outline.
2. Paint the menorah yellow; then set it aside to dry.
3. Cut out the text box and the nine blue candles.
4. Glue the text onto the menorah.
5. Cut out and glue a small orange paper flame to each candle.
6. Glue one candle onto the tall center candleholder to represent the *shammash,* the helper candle.
7. Pretend to light each candle with the shammash and then glue it onto a short candleholder.

Teacher Tips

- To make a tracer, copy the menorah pattern (page 74) onto the left side of a sheet of tagboard, fold the tagboard where indicated, and cut out the pattern through both thicknesses.
- Use paper clips to hold the tracer in place while the child traces it onto the paper plate.

Sue DeRiso—Barrington, RI

Gilded Gelt

Invite each child to create this set of golden gelt coins. Then have students spin a dreidel and show their matching coin. Or have youngsters combine their sets to play a simple memory game.

Materials (per child)

copy of Gelt symbols set (page 75)
4 snap-on plastic milk jug lids
masking tape
gold acrylic paint
paintbrush
scissors
glue

Directions

1. Wrap each milk jug lid with masking tape.
2. Paint each coin gold; then set the coins aside to dry.
3. Cut the four Hebrew symbols apart. Glue a symbol onto the flat side of each gold coin.

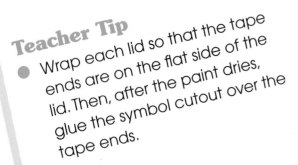

Teacher Tip
● Wrap each lid so that the tape ends are on the flat side of the lid. Then, after the paint dries, glue the symbol cutout over the tape ends.

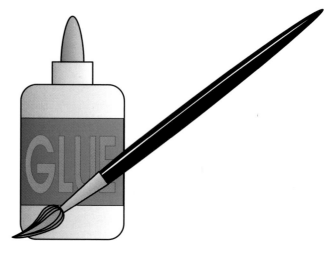

Sue DeRiso—Barrington, RI

Fancy Filter Angel

Enliven the holiday season with this pretty little coffee filter angel. Youngsters might use their angels as hand puppets or as decorative refrigerator magnets.

Materials (per child)

- 2 round coffee filters
- white milk jug lid
- half-length of gold pipe cleaner
- glitter
- cotton
- craft glue
- black permanent marker

Directions

1. Fold one coffee filter in half and glue the edges together.
2. Fold the other coffee filter in half; then fold it in half again and glue the two folded edges together.
3. Glue the folded coffee filters together as shown to create the angel's body.
4. Draw a face inside the milk jug lid; then glue the lid onto the angel's body to resemble the head.
5. Shape the pipe cleaner into a halo. Glue the halo to the back of the head.
6. Glue cotton hair onto the angel's head.
7. Draw a glue design on the angel's body; then sprinkle it with glitter. When the glue is dry, shake off the excess glitter.

glue

glue

Teacher Tips

- To use the angel as a hand puppet, have the child slip her hand into the bottom opening of the angel.
- If desired, attach a piece of magnetic tape to the back of the angel to create a decorative magnet.

Julie A. Koczur

Sock Stocking

Children will hang these stockings with extra special care! After a child completes her stocking, stuff it with a few holiday goodies. Then encourage her to hang her stocking in a special place at home.

Materials (per child)

- child's sock (red or green works best)
- waxed paper
- 5" length of wide ribbon
- 4" length of thin ribbon
- assortment of tiny colorful sequins
- scissors
- craft glue
- permanent marker

Directions

1. Insert a piece of waxed paper into the top of the sock. (This will prevent the glue from seeping through to the opposite side of the sock.)
2. Glue the wide ribbon around the top of the sock. While the glue is still wet, insert the thin ribbon between the sock and wide ribbon to create a hanger.
3. Glue the desired craft items onto the sock.
4. After the glue dries, remove the waxed paper.
5. Use the marker to write your initials on the back of the sock.

Julie A. Koczur

Teacher Tip
- Ask parents to donate new or gently used clean socks for this idea.

Holiday Windsock

Invite each youngster to add this festive windsock to her home holiday decorations to make the season bright.

Materials (per child)

- set of sponge printers (see Teacher Tips)
- 4½" x 20" tagboard strip
- 8–10 wrapping paper strips
- red, green, yellow, and blue tempera paint
- ribbon
- hole puncher
- stapler

Directions

1. Sponge-print holiday shapes onto the tagboard. Allow the paint to dry.
2. Staple eight to ten wrapping paper strips along the bottom of the tagboard.
3. Staple the ends of the tagboard together to create a windsock.
4. Punch a hole near the top of the windsock; then punch another hole opposite the first one.
5. Tie on a ribbon hanger.

Teacher Tips

- To make sponge printers, trace each pattern (page 75) onto a craft sponge; then cut out each shape. Expand the sponge shapes with water and then set them aside to dry.
- As an alternative, trace each shape (page 75) onto thick craft foam. Cut out each shape; then attach a film canister handle to it with craft glue.

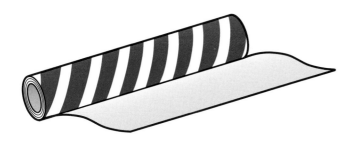

Sue DeRiso—Barrington, RI

Wrapping Paper Wreath

Looking for a creative use for your leftover pieces of wrapping paper? These beautiful wreaths are the perfect solution. Send each child's colorful creation home to enjoy with her family.

Materials (per child)

- paper plate
- large supply of 2" wrapping paper squares
- wide ribbon (or a bow)
- scissors
- tray of glue

Directions

1. Cut out the center of the paper plate to create a ring.
2. Place your index finger in the center of the colorful side of a wrapping paper square. Wrap the paper upward around your finger to create a flower shape.
3. Dip the center of the paper flower into the glue; then press the flower onto the paper plate ring.
4. Repeat Steps 2 and 3 until the ring is covered.
5. After the glue dries, fluff the paper flowers on the wreath.
6. Attach a ribbon bow to the wreath.

Teacher Tips

- Use a large assortment of wrapping paper colors and designs to make a more interesting and colorful wreath.
- Attach a yarn hanger or magnetic tape to the wreath for display purposes.

Julie A. Koczur

Sponge-Print Kinara

Reinforce each youngster's counting and color skills as he sponge-prints the seven candles on this *kinara*, a special candleholder used during the Kwanzaa celebration.

Materials (per child)

- brown kinara (see Teacher Tips)
- large sheet of white construction paper
- black, red, green, and yellow tempera paint
- 3 small sponges
- scissors
- glue
- paintbrush

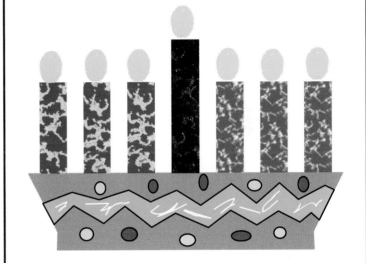

Directions

1. Cut out the kinara pattern; then glue it to the bottom of the white paper.
2. Use the long edge of a sponge to print a tall black candle in the middle of the kinara.
3. Use the short edge of a sponge to sponge-print three red candles to the left of the black candle.
4. In the same manner as in Step 3, print three green candles to the right of the black candle.
5. Top each candle with a yellow fingerprint flame.
6. Paint a design on the kinara.

Teacher Tips

- Enlarge a kinara pattern from page 76; then reproduce it on brown construction paper.
- Use a different sponge for each color of paint.

Margaret Southard—Cleveland, NY

Kwanzaa Beads

On the sixth night of the Kwanzaa celebration, family members often exchange handmade gifts. Invite each child to craft a bead bracelet to give to a family member during a holiday celebration.

Materials

- baking dough (see Teacher Tips)
- wooden chopstick
- cookie sheet
- oven
- red, green, and black tempera paint
- paintbrush
- jute (or black yarn)

Directions

1. Roll a portion of dough into several 1½-inch balls. Gently push and twist each ball onto the chopstick.
2. To dry, place the skewered dough beads on an ungreased cookie sheet and bake them at 200° for three hours.
3. When the beads cool, remove them from the chopstick. Set them aside for about four days to dry thoroughly.
4. Paint each bead the Kwanzaa color of your choice. After the first coat of paint dries, add detail to each bead with another paint color.
5. String the dry beads onto the jute and tie the ends together to create a bracelet.

Teacher Tips

- To make baking dough for 22 beads, mix together 1¼ cups of flour, ¼ cup of salt, and ½ cup of water. Add flour to the mixture as needed until a firm dough forms.
- If an oven is not available, air-dry the skewered dough beads for three days, remove them from the chopstick, and then air-dry them for up to five more days.

Margaret Southard—Cleveland, NY

hat

feather

hat and
cheek circle

Menorah Patterns
Use with "Paper Plate Menorah" on page 65.

candles

text

Hanukkah Lights
See the shining Hanukkah lights,
One bright candle for each night.
Glowing for the world to see—
Happy Hanukkah to you and me!

Place this edge on the fold.

menorah

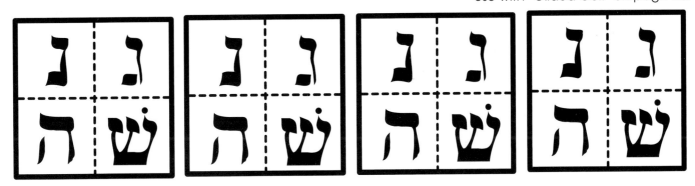

Windsock Patterns
Use with "Holiday Windsock" on page 69.

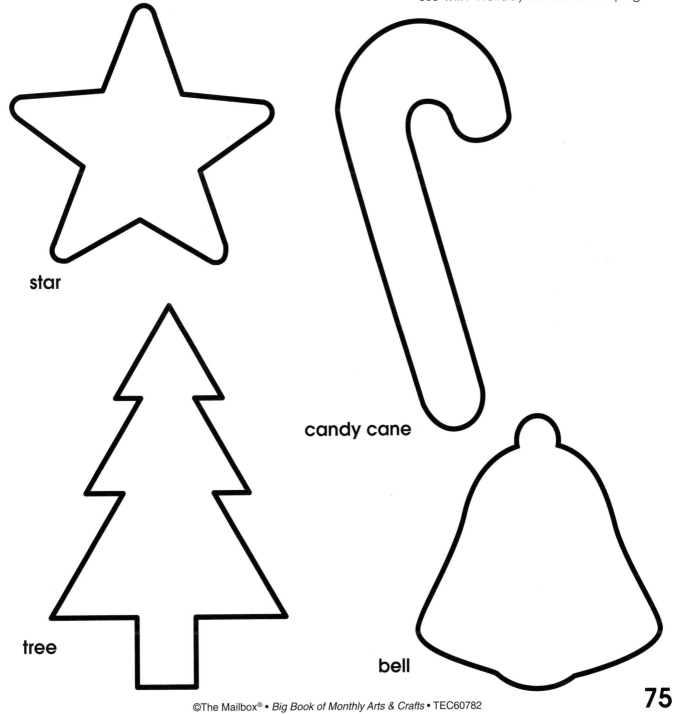

star

candy cane

tree

bell

Kinara Patterns
Use with "Sponge-Print Kinara" on page 71.

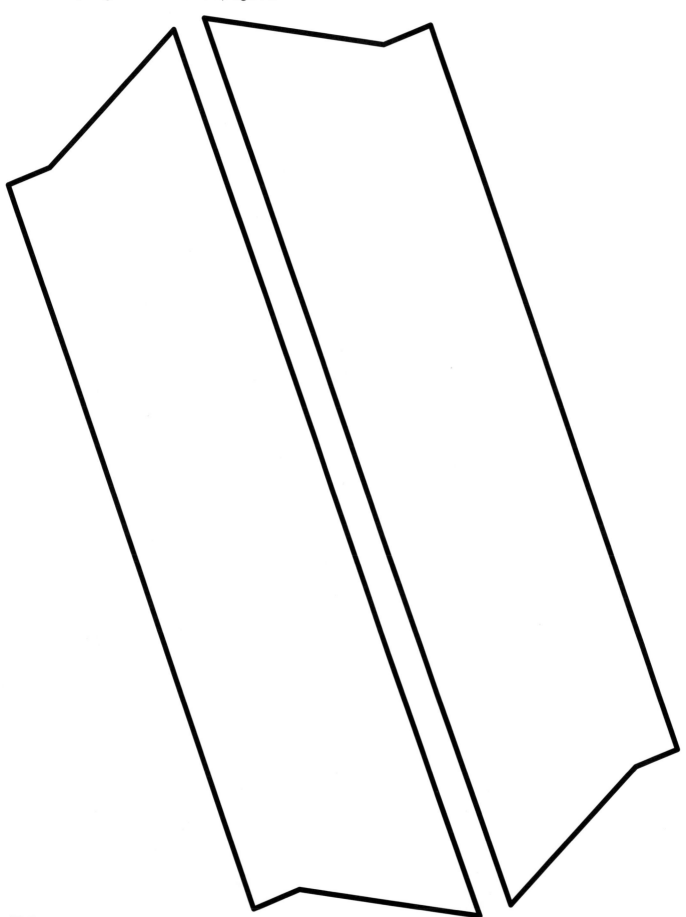

JANUARY

Twelve-Month Mural

Use this simple mural to help each child associate the months of the year with special celebrations and events.

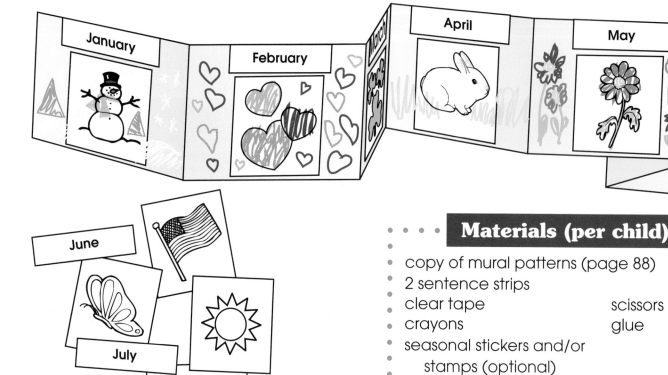

Materials (per child)

- copy of mural patterns (page 88)
- 2 sentence strips
- clear tape   scissors
- crayons   glue
- seasonal stickers and/or stamps (optional)

Teacher Tips

- If desired, laminate each child's mural for durability.
- As an alternative, students might cut out a small magazine picture to represent each month and then glue it onto the corresponding section.

Directions

1. Tape the two sentence strips together to create one long strip.
2. Fold the long strip in half. Then fold it into thirds and then in half again. Unfold the strip to reveal 12 sections.
3. Cut apart each month label and mural picture. Then pair each month with the corresponding picture.
4. Sequence and glue each label-and-picture pair onto a separate section of the sentence strip.
5. After the glue dries, color each picture; then add your own art to each section. Or add a sticker or stamp that represents a special occasion celebrated during that month.

Margaret Southard—Cleveland, NY

Penguin Pencil Holder

Pencils, markers, and rulers will find a cozy resting place in this personalized penguin pencil holder. When the utensils are not in use, have each child store her pencil holder in a designated area in the classroom to create a penguin rookery.

Materials (per child)

- penguin wing, beak, bow, and tie tracers (see Teacher Tips)
- plastic barrel-shaped canister (from powdered soft drink mix)
- black and orange construction paper
- foil wrapping paper
- 2 white hole reinforcers
- black tempera paint (see Teacher Tips)
- white chalk
- permanent marker
- scissors
- craft glue
- paintbrush

Directions

1. Paint the top portion of the canister black and let it dry.
2. Using chalk, outline the wing tracer twice onto black paper; then trace the beak onto orange paper and the bow or tie onto a piece of wrapping paper. Cut out each shape.
3. Use the marker to personalize the bow (or tie).
4. Attach the hole reinforcer eyes, wings, beak, and bow (or tie) as shown.
5. After the glue dries, fold the beak so that it points out.
6. Fill the penguin pencil holder with pencils, markers, rulers, and other utensils of similar length.

Teacher Tips

- To make tracers, cut out tagboard copies of the wing, beak, bow, and tie patterns on page 89.
- Add a few drops of dishwashing liquid to the paint. This will prevent it from peeling off the canister.

Paper Plate Snowflake

Let it snow! Display these beautiful paper plate snowflakes with a wishful snowy title and youngsters will be eager to share their snow wishes with each other. Little ones just can't get enough of that wonderful white fluff!

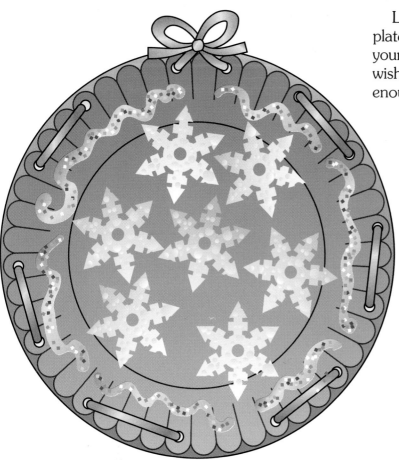

Materials (per child)

- 9" blue paper plate
- snowflake-shaped sponge
- white tempera paint
- silver glitter
- silver ribbon
- hole puncher
- glue

Directions

1. Sponge-paint white snowflakes onto the plate. Allow the paint to dry.
2. Draw glue designs around the edge of the plate; then sprinkle glitter onto the glue.
3. When the glue is dry, punch evenly spaced holes around the plate rim. Then lace the ribbon through the holes.
4. Tie the ends of the ribbon into a bow.

Teacher Tips
- If blue paper plates are not available, you could use a construction paper circle or have each child paint a white paper plate blue.
- For home display purposes, attach a piece of magnetic tape or hot-glue a ribbon loop to the back of each child's paper plate.

adapted from an idea by Julie A. Koczur

Snowpal

This jolly fellow is quite a little "carrot-ter"! Display these special snowpals around your classroom to spread cheer to youngsters throughout the day.

Materials (per child)

- hat, mitten, and boot tracers (see Teacher Tips)
- small white paper plate
- large white paper plate
- black construction paper
- orange bumpy chenille stem section
- pom-poms
- 15" length of ribbon
- wrapping paper   glue
- markers   tape
- scissors   hole puncher

Directions

1. Trace the hat once and the boot twice onto black construction paper. Then trace the mitten twice onto a piece of wrapping paper. Cut out all the shapes.
2. Glue the hat onto the small plate to create the snowpal's head.
3. Draw eyes and a mouth on the face; then poke one end of the chenille piece through the plate to represent a carrot nose. Bend and tape the inserted end to the back of the head.
4. To make the body, glue the mittens and boots onto the large paper plate as shown. Then glue pom-poms onto the body.
5. After the glue dries, punch a hole near the bottom of the head and one near the top of the body. Tie the two sections together with the ribbon.

Teacher Tips
- To make tracers, cut out tagboard copies of the hat, mitten, and boot patterns on page 90.
- To eliminate the sharp point at the end of the chenille nose, fold the tip back onto itself.

Susan Bunyan—Dodge City, KS

Snow Measuring Stick

How deep is the snow on the ground? Or the snow substitute in the sensory table? How tall are my snow boots? How long is my mitten? Invite each child to use this special measuring stick to discover the answers to these questions and more.

Materials (per child)

- 1' wooden paint stirrer
- black felt
- ½" x 8" strip of flannel
- 3 small black pom-poms
- white tempera paint
- black permanent marker
- scissors
- paintbrush
- glue
- ruler

Directions

1. Paint the wooden stirrer white; then set it aside to dry.
2. Cut out a black felt hat and glue it onto the handled end of the stick.
3. Glue the pom-pom eyes and nose onto the stick to create a snowman's face.
4. Cut small snips of felt; then glue them onto the face to represent a mouth.
5. Tie the flannel strip (scarf) around the contoured section of the stick.
6. Starting at the bottom, use the marker and a ruler to mark eight one-inch increments on the stick.
7. Label the back of the stick with "Let It Snow!" and the artist's name.

Teacher Tips
- If desired, put a dot of glue under the scarf to hold it in place.
- To use the full length of the stick for measuring items, label the front with "Let It Snow!"; then label one-inch increments from 1 to 12 on the back.

Sue DeRiso—Barrington, RI

Polar Bear Magnet

Chill out with this friendly polar bear magnet. Encourage each child to take his magnet home to display on his family's refrigerator or any other magnetic surface.

Materials (per child)

- juice can lid (or canning jar lid)
- cotton balls
- 2 small black pom-poms
- large black pom-pom
- about 2" of black pipe cleaner
- magnetic tape
- glue

Directions

1. Gently stretch out several cotton balls; then glue them onto the lid to create the bear's head.
2. To make ears, glue two cotton balls at the top of the head.
3. For the bear's snout, glue two cotton balls side by side in the center of the head.
4. Glue small pom-pom eyes, a large pom-pom nose, and a pipe cleaner mouth onto the head.
5. After the glue dries, attach magnetic tape to the back of the bear.

Teacher Tips

- Shape the pipe cleaner mouth into a wide *W;* then glue it onto the head.
- If desired, lightly dab the center of each ear with red watercolor paint or a pink marker.

Margaret Southard—Cleveland, NY

Winter Rabbit

Every "bunny" in your class will enjoy creating these snow bunny pictures. Display these pictures on a bulletin board covered with quilt batting to enhance the wintry feel.

Materials (per child)

- rabbit tracer (see Teacher Tips)
- half sheet of construction paper (in a bunny color)
- blue construction paper
- cotton balls
- iridescent glitter
- small branchy twig
- white chalk or crayon
- scissors
- water-thinned glue
- paintbrush
- glue

Directions

1. Glue a row of cotton balls along the bottom edge of the paper to represent a snow-covered ground.
2. Use chalk to outline the rabbit tracer on the half sheet of construction paper. Cut out the rabbit; then glue it on the snow-covered ground.
3. Glue the twig along one side of the paper so that it resembles a tree or bush.
4. To make snowflakes, use scissors to snip a cotton ball into small pieces. Fluff each snowflake.
5. Paint water-thinned glue over the entire picture; then lightly sprinkle the cotton snowflakes and glitter onto the glue to create a wintry scene.

Teacher Tips
- To make a tracer, cut out a tagboard copy of the rabbit pattern on page 89.
- To make water-thinned glue, mix equal amounts of glue and water.
- In advance, bundle youngsters up and take them on a winter nature walk to collect twigs for this activity.

Mackie Rhodes—Greensboro, NC

Beautiful Bird

Convert a simple paper plate into a beautiful bird! Then display these lovely creatures to cheer up the winter scenery in your classroom.

Materials (per child)

- bird tracer (see Teacher Tips)
- 9" white paper plate
- blue, brown, or red tempera paint
- gray tempera paint
- 2 white hole reinforcers
- ribbon   glue
- newspaper   paintbrush
- marker
- scissors

Directions

1. Paint the front of the plate with the color of your choice; then set it aside to dry.
2. Turn the plate over and then paint the back of the plate with the same color.
3. Crumple a piece of newspaper into a loose ball. Dip the ball into gray paint and lightly blot the front of the plate with it. Let it dry.
4. Turn the plate over and repeat Step 3.
5. After the paint dries, fold the plate in half toward the back. Fit the bird tracer to the folded plate as shown; then trace it onto the plate.
6. Cut out the bird outline through both thicknesses of the plate.
7. Glue the head and body sections together (as shown), leaving the wings and tail free. Insert a loop of ribbon into the glue as shown.
8. Attach a hole reinforcer eye to each side of the head.
9. After the glue dries, spread the wings and tail so that the bird appears to be flying.

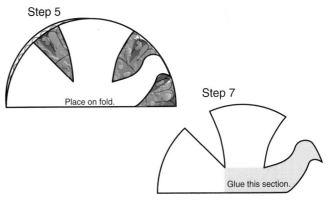

Step 5

Place on fold.

Step 7

Glue this section.

Teacher Tips

- Cut out a tagboard copy of the bird pattern on page 91 to make a tracer.
- Clip a clothespin onto the head and body sections to hold them together while the glue dries.
- To make a peace dove, simply blot gray paint onto the white paper plate; then follow Steps 5–9.

Mackie Rhodes—Greensboro, NC

Dragon Hand Puppet

Invite youngsters to parade these colorful dragon puppets around your school to celebrate the start of a great new year!

Step 5

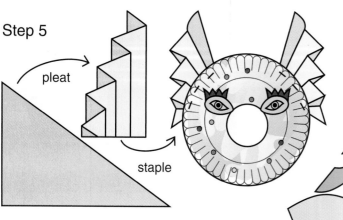

pleat

staple

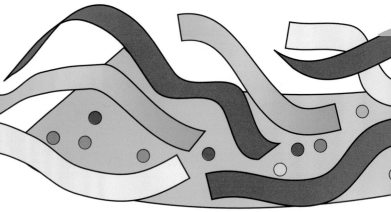

Steps 6 and 7

knotted ribbon

dot nostrils

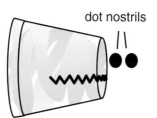

Step 9

glue to cup

ribbon

tail

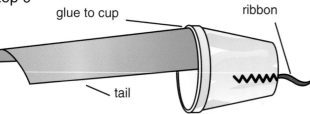

Teacher Tips

- To make glue-paint, mix two parts glue with one part tempera paint.
- Use clothespins to hold the tail on the cup while the glue dries.

Materials (per child)

- green construction paper eye patterns (page 92)
- red construction paper eyelash patterns (page 92)
- 8 oz. polystyrene cup
- 9" paper plate
- 2 half sheets of green construction paper (cut lengthwise)
- 2 half sheets of yellow construction paper (cut diagonally)
- assorted widths and colors of ribbon and tissue paper strips
- green and yellow glue-paint (see Teacher Tips)
- two ½" black construction paper dots
- 3" length of red ribbon
- glitter
- tiny sequins
- permanent marker
- paintbrush
- scissors
- stapler
- glue

Julie Koczur

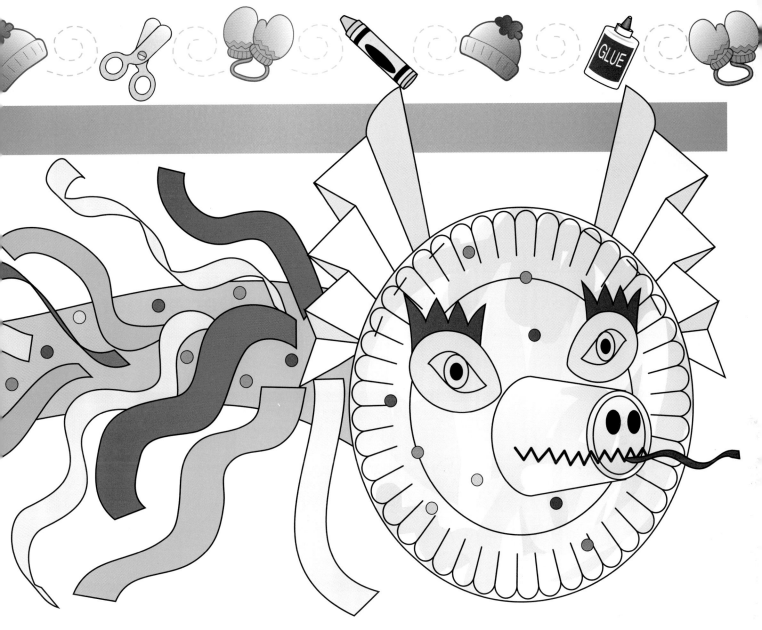

Directions

1. Cut out the eye and eyelash patterns. Glue an eyelash onto each eye.
2. To make the head, cut out a three-inch circle from the middle of the plate.
3. Paint the back of the plate with both glue-paint colors. Sprinkle glitter onto the wet paint.
4. After the paint dries on the back, paint and glitter the front of the plate. Add sequins and press the eyes onto the wet glue. Set the plate aside to dry.
5. Pleat each yellow triangle to create winged ears; then staple each ear onto the plate as shown.
6. Paint and glitter the cup; then press two paper nostrils into the wet glue on the bottom of the cup. After the glue dries, draw a mouth on the cup with the marker.
7. Poke a small hole in the bottom of the cup. Knot one end of the red ribbon; then insert the other end through the hole to make a tongue.
8. Tape the green paper halves together to make a long tail strip. Glue ribbon, tissue paper strips, and sequins onto the tail.
9. Glue one end of the tail around the cup rim opposite the paper nostrils.
10. Edge the hole in the plate with glue. Fit the cup snugly into the hole; then let the glue dry.

Month Labels and Mural Pictures

Use with "Twelve-Month Mural" on page 78.

January	February	March
April	May	June
July	August	September
October	November	December

wing

bow

tie

beak

Rabbit Pattern
Use with "Winter Rabbit" on page 84.

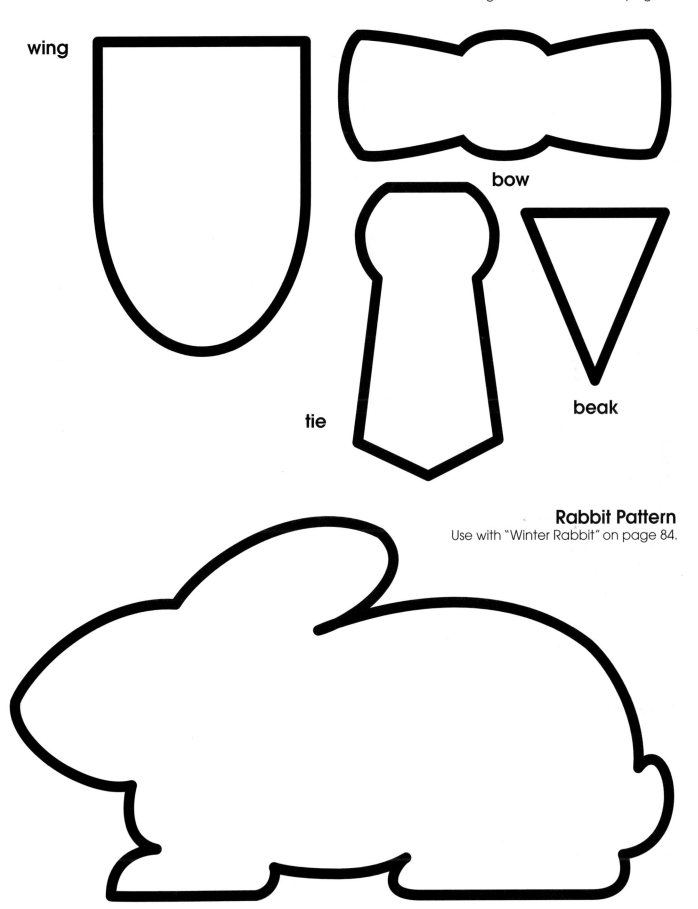

Snowpal Patterns
Use with "Snowpal" on page 81.

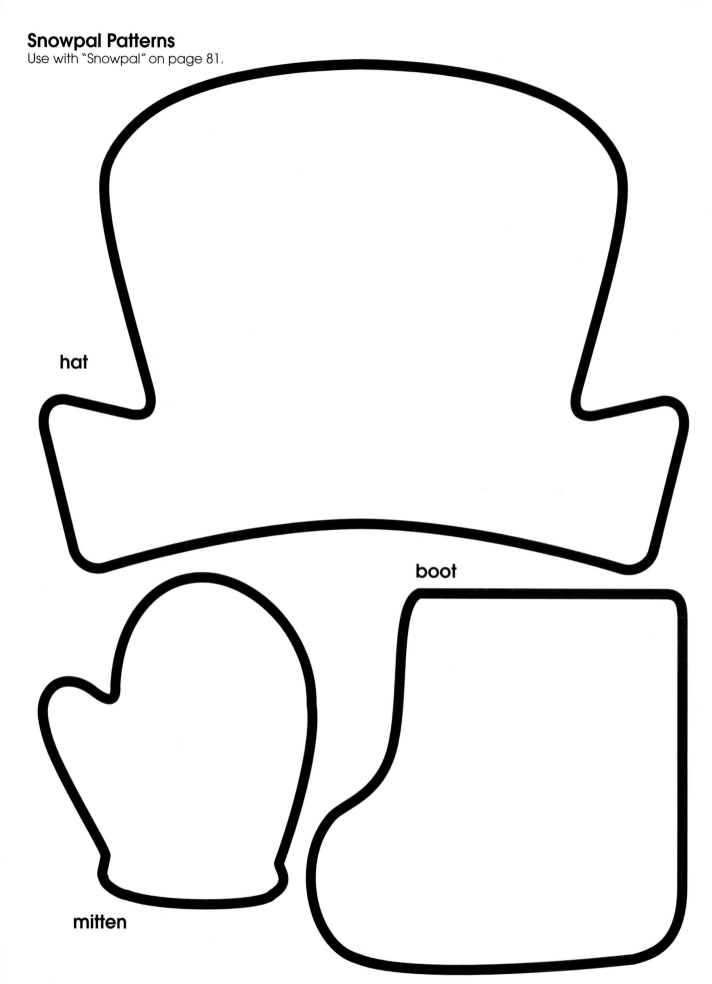

hat

boot

mitten

90

Place on fold.

Dragon Patterns
Use with "Dragon Hand Puppet" on pages 86–87.

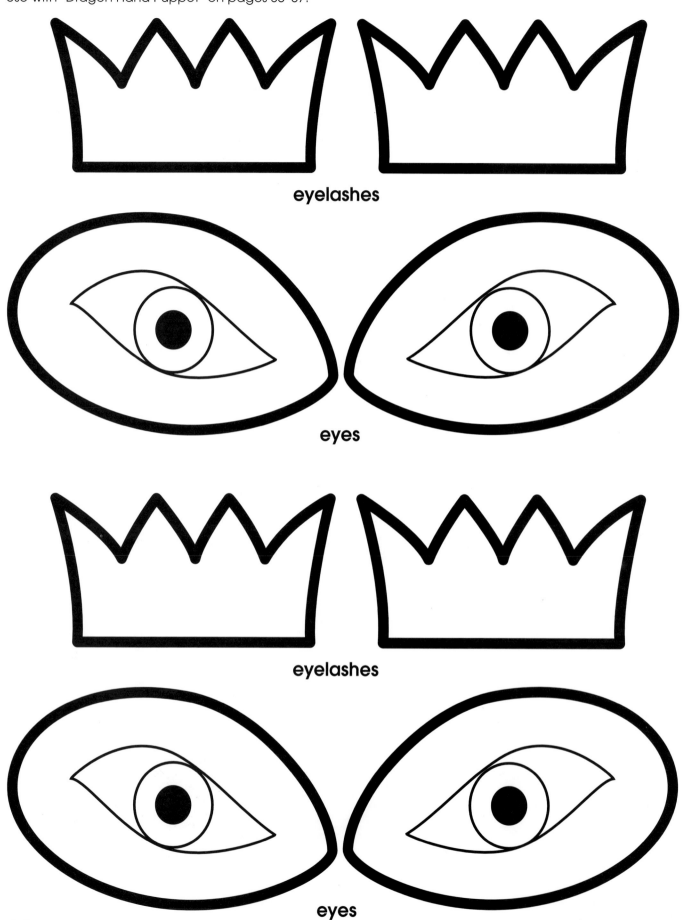

eyelashes

eyes

eyelashes

eyes

92

FEBRUARY

Groundhog Garden

¾" pom-poms

1" pom-poms

Is spring just around the corner or will winter linger on? These groundhog planters will help your little ones forecast the weather and start their spring planting, too!

Early Spring

More Winter

Materials (per child)

- 2½" brown craft foam circle
- two ¾" brown pom-poms (ears)
- two 1" brown pom-poms (paws)
- black mini pom-pom (nose)
- 2 white hole reinforcers
- spring-type clothespin
- red craft foam   crayons
- 8-oz. foam cup   black permanent
- soil   marker
- seeds   scissors
- pencil   craft glue

Directions

1. To make a groundhog, attach the hole-reinforcer eyes and black nose onto the foam circle.
2. Cut out a red foam mouth; then glue it onto the groundhog.
3. To make ears and paws, glue the pom-poms onto the groundhog as shown.
4. On one side of the cup, use the black marker to draw a groundhog shadow. Write "More Winter" near the shadow.
5. Use crayons to draw flowers on the opposite side of the cup. Write "Early Spring" near the flowers.
6. Fill the planter with soil; then plant a few seeds in the soil.
7. Glue the groundhog to a clothespin. After the glue dries, clip the clothespin to the planter.

Teacher Tips

- If desired, substitute construction paper for the craft foam.
- Plant seeds that have a short germination period, such as grass or marigolds.
- On Groundhog Day, set the planter outdoors to see whether or not it casts a shadow. Attach the groundhog to the corresponding side.

Julie Koczur

"Heart-y" Groundhog

There's one thing for sure—this little guy's got a lot of heart! Display these lovable critters on a bulletin board to greet the month of February.

Materials (per child)

- tagboard heart tracers (see Teacher Tips)
- white construction copy of the small paper heart pattern (page 108)
- white construction paper copy of the eyes pattern (page 107)
- large sheet of brown construction paper
- black construction paper
- 3" lengths of white pipe cleaner
- markers
- scissors
- glue

Step 2

Directions

1. Fold the brown construction paper in half. Place the straight edge of the large half-heart tracer on the fold; then trace it and cut it out. *Do not cut on the fold.*
2. To make ears, trace the smaller heart tracer on brown paper. Cut out the heart; then cut it in half (each half will be an ear).
3. Cut out a black construction paper nose. Then cut out the eyes and the small white heart (for teeth).
4. Glue the ears, eyes, nose, and teeth onto the large heart as shown. Then glue on pipe cleaner whiskers.
5. Use markers to add details to the groundhog.

Margaret Southard—Cleveland, NY

Teacher Tips

- To make tracers, cut out tagboard copies of the large half heart pattern on page 107 and the small heart pattern on page 108.
- If desired, glue a wide craft stick to the groundhog to make a puppet.
- To convert this project into a mask, cut out eyeholes instead of gluing eyes on the face. Then add a wide craft stick handle.

95

Tooth Fairy Box

Invite each child to create this sparkling tooth box to take home. Encourage him to use the box to safely hold his little white gems as he awaits the tooth fairy's visit.

While I'm in bed
And soundly sleeping,
I put my tooth here
For safekeeping.

Materials (per child)

- white construction paper copy of the tooth pattern and text cloud (page 108)
- individual-size milk carton
- white glue paint (see Teacher Tips)
- brad
- 5" length of pipe cleaner
- glitter
- scissors
- paintbrush
- hole puncher
- clear tape
- glue

Step 1   Step 3   Steps 4 and 5

  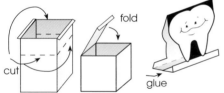 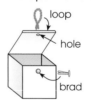

cut   fold   glue   loop   hole   brad

Directions

1. Pull open all sides of the milk carton top. Cut off three sides of the top, leaving one side to use as a fold-down lid (as shown).
2. Paint the outside of the carton with white glue paint; then sprinkle glitter on the wet paint. Let it dry.
3. Cut out the tooth pattern and text cloud. Fold the tooth cutout in half and at both ends where indicated. Glue the folded ends together to make a stand-up figure (as shown).
4. Punch a hole one-half inch from the top of the box front. Secure the brad in the hole; then tape the brad ends in place.
5. Make a pipe cleaner loop. Poke the ends of the loop into the box lid. To secure the loop, spread the ends out and tape them in place.
6. Glue the stand-up tooth on the box lid.
7. Glue the text cloud on the front. Let the glue dry.
8. To use, put a lost tooth in the box. Close the lid and hook the loop over the brad.

Teacher Tips

- To make glue paint, mix equal amounts of white paint and glue.
- If necessary, poke a pushpin in the lid to start the hole for the pipe cleaner loop.
- Use a large paper clip to hold the tooth in place on the lid while the glue dries.

Sue DeRiso—Barrington, RI

George Washington Hat

To celebrate Presidents' Day, invite each child to make and proudly wear this patriotic, three-cornered hat. What a perfect prop for a parade or for dramatic-play activities.

Materials (per child)

- construction paper copy of the hat pattern (page 109) in each color: red, white, blue
- yellow construction paper copy of the medallion pattern (page 109)
- red craft feather
- scissors
- glue
- stapler

Step 2

Directions

1. Cut out the medallion and each hat pattern.
2. Poke the end of the feather through the blue hat pattern as shown.
3. Glue the medallion over the feather and let the glue dry.
4. Staple one end of the blue hat to one end of the red hat. Then staple the other end of the blue hat to the white hat.
5. Staple the loose ends of the white and red hats together.

Teacher Tips

- If needed, use a pushpin to start the holes in the blue hat; then insert the feather.
- As you staple the ends together, adjust the hat to fit the child's head.

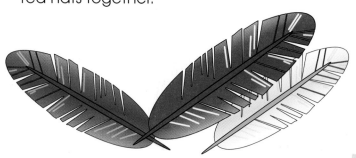

Susan Bunyan—Dodge City, KS

Lincoln Look-Alike Mask

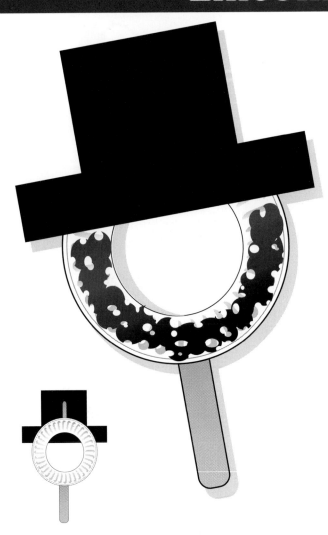

Enhance your Presidents' Day unit with these Abraham Lincoln masks. During group time, invite each child to don her mask as she shares a Lincoln fact with the class.

Materials (per child)

- 9" paper plate
- sheet of black construction paper
- wide craft stick
- cotton balls
- black tempera paint
- scissors
- glue

Directions

1. Cut out the center of the paper plate, creating a ring from the plate rim.
2. Use cotton balls to dab black paint around the rim. Let the paint dry.
3. Fold the black paper in half; then cut out a stovepipe hat shape as shown.
4. Glue the hat to the top of the painted ring.
5. Glue a craft stick handle to the back of the ring.

Teacher Tips

- Use a clothespin to hold the handle in place while the glue dries.
- If necessary, to reinforce the hat so that it stands up, slide a regular craft stick between the plate rim and the hat; then glue it in place.

Sue DeRiso—Barrington, RI

Woven Heart Pocket

Little fingers weave lots of love into this special heart pocket. Invite each child to use his pocket to collect valentines. Or have him fill it with an edible treat to give to a loved one.

Materials (per child)

- large tagboard heart tracers (see Teacher Tips)
- white poster board
- red poster board
- seasonal ribbons
- scissors
- decorative edging scissors
- glue
- pencil

Directions

1. Trace the larger heart onto white poster board. Cut it out with decorative scissors.
2. Trace the smaller heart onto red poster board; then cut it out.
3. Fold the red heart in half. Cut slits in the heart as shown, spacing them one-half inch apart.
4. Unfold the heart and then weave lengths of ribbon through the slits in an alternating pattern. Trim the excess ribbon.
5. Glue the edges of the red heart to the white heart, leaving the top open to create a pocket.

Step 3

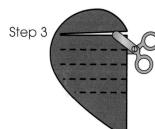

Teacher Tips

- To make tracers, cut out two tagboard hearts, one slightly smaller than the other. If desired, use the large half-heart pattern on page 107 as a guide for the tracers.
- If desired, add a ribbon loop to the back of the pocket for display purposes.

Julie Koczur

Bouquet of Love

This vase full of happy hearts and beautiful blooms is the perfect gift for each child to present to a special loved one.

Materials (per child)

- tagboard heart and flower tracers (see Teacher Tips)
- laundry detergent bottle lid
- pipe cleaners (cut about 1" longer than the lid height)
- polystyrene foam block cut to fit inside the lid
- pink, white, and red craft foam
- pencil with blunt point (or ballpoint pen)
- seasonal or red ribbon
- heart confetti or punch-outs
- scissors
- craft glue

Directions

1. To make a vase, decorate the lid with the ribbon and heart confetti.
2. Trace several hearts and/or flowers on the craft foam; then cut out each shape. Use a pencil to make a pilot hole in each.
3. Gently poke one end of a pipe cleaner into each cutout.
4. Use the pencil to poke one hole (per flower) into the foam block. Then insert the free end of each pipe cleaner into the foam block.
5. Press the foam block firmly into the bottom of the vase.
6. Spread out, bend, and turn the hearts and/or blooms to arrange

Teacher Tips

- To make tracers, draw a few different heart and flower sizes onto tagboard; then cut them out. If desired, copy a few different sizes of the small heart pattern (page 108) onto tagboard; then cut them out.
- If desired, invite children to embellish the hearts and blooms with glitter, sequins, and seasonal confetti before putting them in the foam block.

Margaret Southard—Cleveland, NY

Valentine Box

This pretty valentine box is durable and easy to use. Have youngsters drop their valentines in the corresponding boxes. Then, during your valentine celebration, invite each child to open the flap on his box to retrieve his special messages.

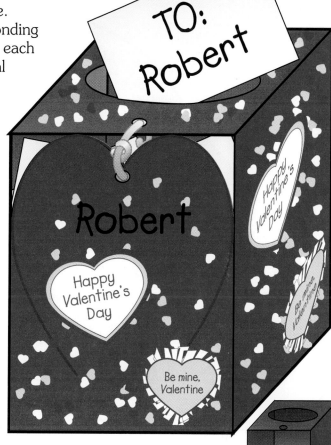

Materials (per child)

- covered cube-shaped tissue box (see Teacher Tip)
- tempera paint (to match or complement the covered box color)
- seasonal confetti, stickers, and assorted heart cutouts
- 2 ½" length of pipe cleaner
- craft knife (for teacher use)
- paintbrush
- scissors
- permanent marker
- craft glue
- hole puncher

Directions

1. Paint the top of the tissue box. Let the paint dry.
2. Use the marker to write your name on the flap.
3. Decorate the box with valentine confetti, stickers, and heart cutouts.
4. Punch a hole in the box top and another in the flap as shown.
5. Thread one end of the pipe cleaner through the hole in the flap; then twist it to secure it.
6. Shape the other end of the pipe cleaner into a hook. Insert it into the hole in the box top.
7. To use, deposit valentine cards (and small treats) in the top opening of the box. Then unhook and open the flap to remove the goodies.

Ada Goren—Winston Salem, NC

Teacher Tip
- In advance, cover the sides of the box with a 5½" x 18" piece of red, pink, or white Con-Tact covering. Use the craft knife to cut along the edges as shown. Then cut out a heart-shaped flap with scissors.

Candy Kiss

This giant candy kiss will get your youngsters in the mood for the real thing! So surprise each child with a real candy kiss after she completes this project!

Materials (per child)

- tagboard candy kiss tracer (see Teacher Tip)
- white construction paper
- sheet of tagboard
- 12" square of aluminum foil
- permanent markers
- scissors
- glue
- tape

Directions

1. Fold the sheet of tagboard in half. Place the straight edge of the tracer on the fold; then trace it and cut it out. *Do not cut on the fold.*
2. Unfold the kiss cutout. Then gently wrap the foil, shiny side up, around the kiss. Glue the edges of the foil to the back.
3. Cut out a ribbon shape from white construction paper. Tape the ribbon to the back of the kiss.
4. Use markers to write your name on the ribbon and to draw a face on the candy.

Teacher Tip
- To make a tracer, cut out a tagboard copy of the candy kiss pattern on page 108.

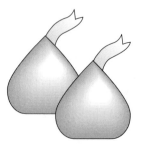

Susan Bunyan—Dodge City, KS

Lovely Suncatcher

Warm up your classroom with these lovely creations! Throughout February, display the suncatchers in your classroom window to capture the beauty of the winter sun.

Materials (per child)

- tagboard heart tracer (see Teacher Tips)
- 2 large sheets of red construction paper
- 12" x 15" piece of clear Con-Tact covering
- tissue paper hearts in assorted colors and sizes (see Teacher Tips)
- clear glitter
- pencil
- scissors
- craft glue

Directions

1. To make heart rings, fold each sheet of red construction paper in half. Place the straight edge of the heart tracer on the fold of each sheet; then trace the outer and inner edges of it. Cut out the shape on both lines. *Do not cut on the fold.*
2. Fold the Con-Tact covering in half. Place the straight edge of the heart tracer on the fold. Trace *only* the outer edge of the tracer with a pencil; then cut out the shape.
3. Remove the backing from the Con-Tact covering. Randomly place tissue paper hearts on the sticky side of the covering.
4. Sprinkle glitter onto the remaining sticky areas of the covering.
5. Glue the decorated covering between the two heart rings.

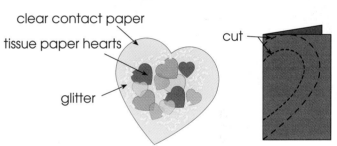

clear contact paper

tissue paper hearts

glitter

cut

Teacher Tips

- To make a heart tracer, cut out a tagboard copy of the large half-heart pattern (page 107). Then, starting and ending on the straight edge, cut 1½ inches inside the curve of the shape. (Use this tracer for the heart rings in Step 1 and the heart in Step 2.)
- If desired, enlarge and reduce the small heart pattern on page 108; then use the different heart sizes as guides to cut out tissue paper hearts.

Julie Koczur

103

Valentine Puzzle

This bundle of sticks holds a clever little surprise—a valentine puzzle! Ask each child to challenge a friend to assemble her sticks to discover the special valentine greeting.

Materials (per child)

- 6 wide craft sticks
- markers
- masking tape
- red or pink ribbon

Directions

1. Tape the craft sticks together to create a panel as shown.
2. Turn the panel over. Use markers to draw a valentine picture and/or write a special message on the panel.
3. Remove the tape from the back of the panel to separate the sticks.
4. Stack the sticks in random order; then tie a ribbon around them.
5. To use, unwrap the sticks; then put them together to display the picture and/or greeting.

Teacher Tip

- As an alternative to tying the sticks together with ribbon, invite the child to decorate a white envelope; then have her put the sticks in it.

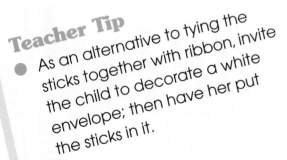

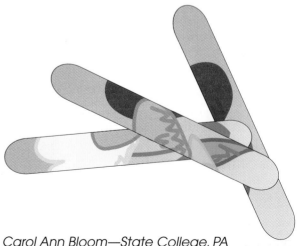

Carol Ann Bloom—State College, PA

Wonderful Whales

Your little ones will have a lot to spout about when they create these models of whales. Invite each child to show off her whale as she shares her knowledge of this fascinating mammal with the class.

Materials (per child)

- construction paper copy of the whale patterns (page 110)
- construction paper scraps
- small paper bag
- newspaper scraps
- tempera paint (in any whale color)
- paintbrush
- scissors
- masking tape
- clear tape
- glue

Directions

1. Half-fill the bag with newspaper scraps. Twist the middle of the bag to close it; then wrap masking tape around the twisted section.
2. Paint the bag. Allow the paint to dry.
3. Cut out the flipper, eyes, and spout patterns. Also cut out a mouth shape. Fold the spout where indicated.
4. Glue the eyes, mouth, and spout onto the bag as shown.
5. Cut the flipper in half. Glue half a flipper to each side of the whale, using clear tape to hold each one in place.

Teacher Tip
- Use a pushpin to hold the spout in place while the glue dries.

Sue DeRiso—Barrington, RI

Paper Plate Orca

Try this whale of an idea to add interest and fun to your whales unit. Then display these awesome orcas on an underwater background.

Materials (per child)

- tagboard fin, flipper, and belly tracers (see Teacher Tips)
- three 6" paper plates
- black construction paper
- red construction paper scraps
- 2 small black pom-poms
- white chalk
- black tempera paint
- paintbrush
- scissors
- glue
- pencil

Directions

1. Paint the bottom of one paper plate black and let it dry.
2. With the insides facing together, glue the rim of the painted plate to the second plate to make the whale's body. (The front is black and the back is white.)
3. Fit the belly tracer to the curve of the third plate. Trace and cut out the belly.
4. Cut out a red paper wedge to fit the inside curve of the belly. Glue the wedge in place to serve as a mouth.
5. Use chalk to outline the fin and flipper tracers on black paper. Cut out each shape.
6. Glue the fin and flipper to the back of the whale. Then glue the belly and two black pom-pom eyes to the front of the whale.

Margaret Southard—Cleveland, NY

Teacher Tips

- To make tracers, cut out a tagboard copy of the orca patterns (fin, flipper, and belly) on page 110.
- Use clothespins to hold the plates together while the glue dries.

Place on fold.

Eye Pattern
Use with "'Heart-y' Groundhog" on page 95.

Tooth Pattern and Text Cloud

Use with "Tooth Fairy Box" on page 96.

Fold.

Fold.

While I'm in bed
And soundly sleeping,
I put my tooth here
For safekeeping.

Place on fold.

Candy Kiss Pattern
Use with "Candy Kiss" on page 102.

Small Heart Pattern
Use with "'Heart-y' Groundhog" on page 95 and
"Lovely Suncatcher" on page 103.

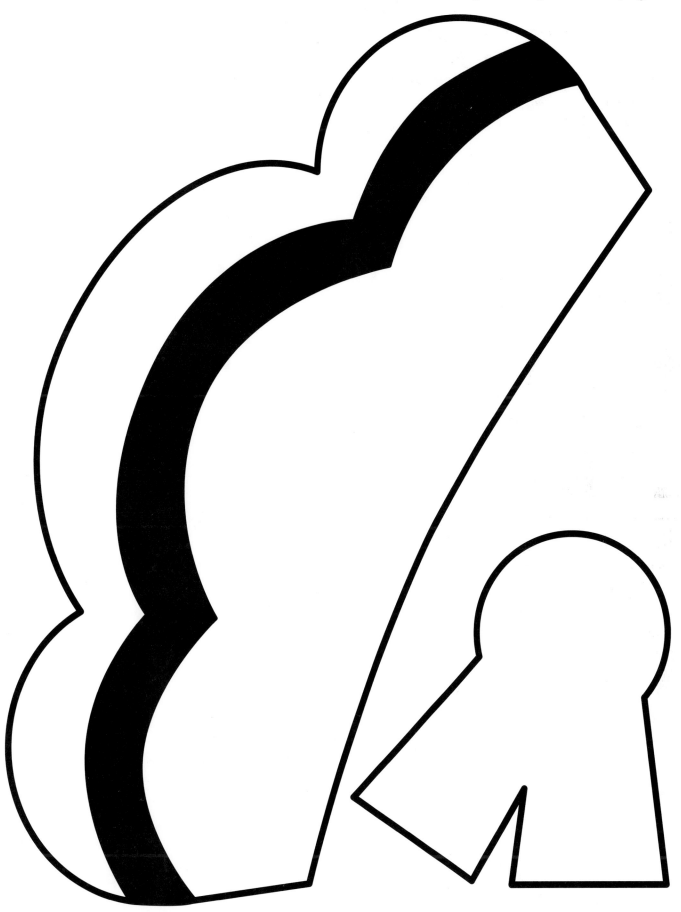

Orca Patterns

Use with "Paper Plate Orca" on page 106. Also use the flipper pattern with "Wonderful Whales" on page 105.

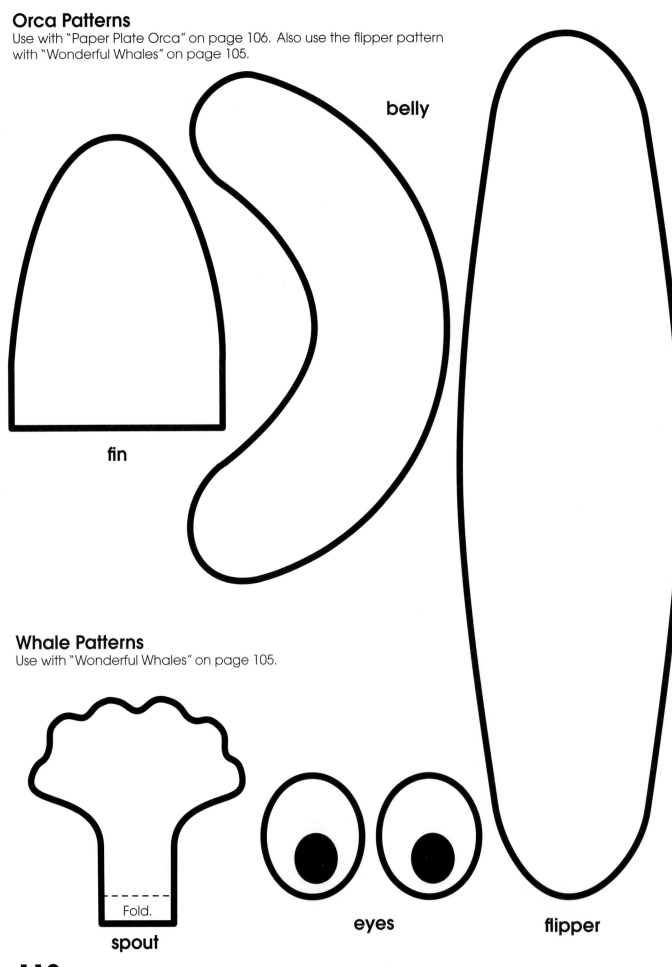

belly

fin

Whale Patterns

Use with "Wonderful Whales" on page 105.

Fold.

spout

eyes

flipper

MARCH

Weather Wheel

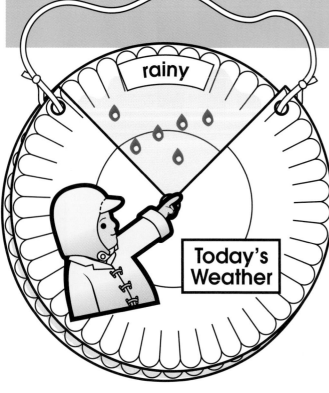

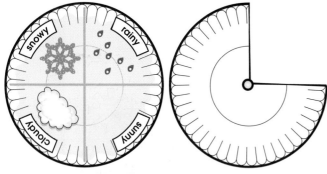

Display these weather wheels in your classroom. Then invite each child to turn his wheel to the appropriate weather for each day.

Materials (per child)

- weather wheel patterns (page 122)
- two 9" paper plates
- sun stencil (see Teacher Tip)
- sponge snowflake
- light blue, dark blue, and yellow tempera paints
- silver glitter
- cotton balls
- cotton swab
- 18" length of ribbon
- permanent marker
- brad
- scissors
- glue
- hole puncher
- crayons

Directions

1. Cut out the patterns. Color the weatherperson.
2. Cut out a quarter section of one paper plate.
3. Use the marker to divide the other paper plate into quarters. With a cotton ball, lightly paint the entire plate light blue, leaving the lines visible. Let the paint dry.
4. Use a cotton ball to stencil a yellow sun on one section of the plate.
5. Use the cotton swab to dot dark blue raindrops on another section.
6. Glue a stretched-out cotton ball cloud to a third section.
7. Sponge-paint a dark blue snowflake on the last section; then sprinkle glitter on the wet paint.
8. Glue each weather word to the corresponding section.
9. When the project is dry, stack the plates and attach the two plates with the brad. Then glue the weatherperson and the title on the top plate.
10. Punch a hole on each side of the opening on the top plate; then attach the ribbon.

Susan DeRiso—Barrington, RI

Teacher Tip

- To make a durable sun stencil, cut out a sun shape from the center of a four-inch (or smaller) plastic lid.

Lion-Lamb Flip Masks

March winds might be as fierce as a lion at one moment and as gentle as a lamb the next. To help youngsters relate to this concept, have them role-play these two animals with this unique flip mask.

Materials (per child)

- two 9" paper plates
- brown and black (or gray) construction paper scraps
- supply of 4" lengths of yellow, brown, or orange crepe paper
- cotton balls
- yarn
- glue
- scissors
- hole puncher

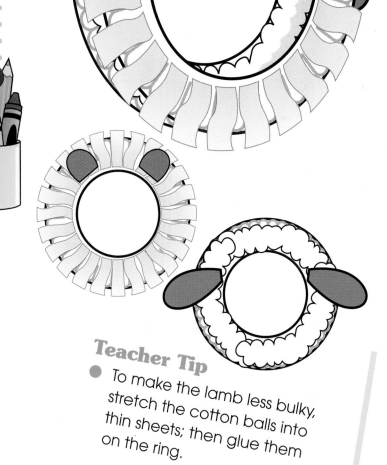

Directions

1. Cut out the center of each plate to create a ring.
2. Cut out two lion ears and two lamb ears.
3. To make a lion, glue crepe paper strips around one of the paper plate rings so that it resembles a mane. Glue the lion ears onto the mane.
4. To make a lamb, glue cotton balls around the other ring. Glue the lamb ears onto the lamb's head.
5. Stack the two masks; then punch two holes in the top of each one. Tie them together with yarn.
6. To use, flip the desired mask to the front; then hold it up to your face.

Teacher Tip
● To make the lamb less bulky, stretch the cotton balls into thin sheets; then glue them on the ring.

Mackie Rhodes—Greensboro, NC

Rainbow Table Topper

Top off your rainbow studies with this decorative table topper. Encourage each child to take her completed project home to share her rainbow knowledge with her family.

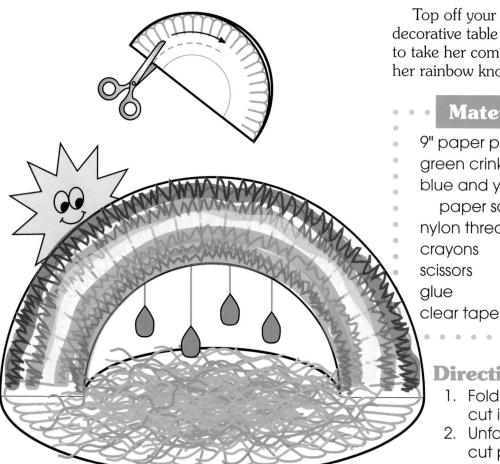

Materials (per child)

9" paper plate
green crinkle strips (or Easter grass)
blue and yellow construction
   paper scraps
nylon thread
crayons
scissors
glue
clear tape

Directions

1. Fold the paper plate in half and cut it as shown.
2. Unfold the plate; then color the cut part of the rim to resemble a rainbow.
3. Cut out a few small blue raindrops and a yellow sun.
4. Tape the end of a short length of nylon thread to each raindrop. Then tape the other end of the thread to the back of the rainbow to suspend each raindrop.
5. Glue the sun to the rainbow as shown.
6. Fold the rainbow forward so that it stands up.
7. Glue the crinkle strips onto the bottom of the plate; then set it aside to dry.

Teacher Tips

● To guide the child in coloring her rainbow, dot each end of the rainbow with this sequence of colors: red, orange, yellow, green, blue, and purple.

● Have children practice telling each other how the sun and rain work together to create a real rainbow. Then encourage each child to share the same information with her family.

Mackie Rhodes—Greensboro, NC

Shamrock Note Holder

Praise behaviors, reinforce learning, or just spread smiles with this fun idea. Have each child clip her special shamrock messages to her note holder for safekeeping. Later, have her take her clip full of notes home to share with her family.

Materials (per child)

- spring-type clothespin
- small construction paper or felt shamrock
- white construction paper
- shamrock sponge printer
- ½"-wide seasonal ribbon
- green tempera paint
- glitter (optional)
- scissors
- glue
- magnetic tape

Thanks for being such a good helper today!

Directions

1. To make the note holder, glue a length of ribbon onto one side of the clothespin.
2. If desired, glue glitter on the small shamrock. Then glue that shamrock to the note holder as shown.
3. Attach a piece of magnetic tape to the other side of the note holder; then display it on a magnetic surface.
4. Sponge-paint a few shamrocks on white paper. When the glue is dry, cut out the shapes. Ask friends and adults to write special messages on your shamrocks.
5. Collect your shamrocks and then clip them to your note holder.

Teacher Tips

- If a shamrock sponge is not available, use a small heart sponge instead. To make a shamrock shape, simply sponge-paint three hearts that touch at the points.

Julie Koczur

Lucky Leprechaun Hat

Dress up your St. Patrick's Day celebration with this whimsical hat. Be sure to invite each child to tuck a few shamrocks into her hatband just for the luck of it!

Materials (per child)

green plastic bowl
16" length of ½"-wide seasonal ribbon
two 18" lengths of yarn
green construction paper
green and gold glitter
scissors
glue
paintbrush
clear acrylic spray
hole puncher

Directions

1. Paint a coat of glue over the entire back of the bowl.
2. Sprinkle green and gold glitter on the glue; then let it dry.
3. To prevent the glitter from flaking off, spray the hat with clear acrylic spray.
4. Cut out one or more small shamrocks from green paper (see Teacher Tips).
5. Squeeze a line of glue along the back of the ribbon; then arrange the ribbon around the hat to create a hatband.
6. While the glue is still wet, tuck the stem of each shamrock between the hatband and hat.
7. To make ties for the hat, punch two holes in the hat brim; then tie a length of yarn to each hole.

Julie Koczur

Teacher Tips

- For variety, invite each child to embellish her hat with seasonal stickers.
- If desired, copy the shamrock pattern (page 122) on green construction paper. Have the child cut out the shamrocks for her hat.

Dainty Dandelion

Show off these colorful dandelions in a brilliant spring display. Later, back them with magnetic tape to create decorative magnets for youngsters to share with their families.

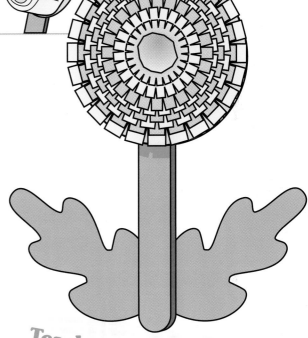

Materials (per child)

- white soda bottle lid
- 2" tagboard circle
- green construction paper
- sheet of yellow tissue paper
- green craft stick
- glue
- scissors
- stapler

Directions

1. Fold the tissue paper in half lengthwise. Fold it in half three more times or until the width is about 1½ inches.
2. Staple about every inch along the folded edge of the tissue paper. Squeeze a line of glue along the same edge.
3. Starting at one end, roll the strip around the bottle lid. Then secure the end of the strip with glue.
4. Glue the wrapped bottle lid to the circle. Then glue the circle to one end of the craft stick.
5. Cut out two green dandelion leaves and glue them to the stem.
6. After the glue dries, fringe the top of the dandelion. Then gently spread and fluff the fringed ends.

Teacher Tips

- Use a clothespin to hold the end of the paper strip in place while the glue dries.
- To make a green craft stick, color a wooden craft stick with a green permanent marker.
- To make a two-sided dandelion, repeat Steps 1–3 and 6, gluing the dandelion to the back of the first one. If desired, use white tissue paper to show the two phases of this interesting plant.

Mackie Rhodes—Greensboro, NC

Spring Flowers

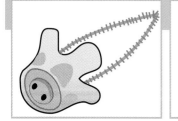

Hints of spring are in the air! Invite youngsters to create these pretty spring flowers in celebration of the burst of blooms where you live.

Materials (per child)

- several cardboard egg-carton cups
- assorted colors of tempera paint
- assorted colors of tissue paper
- green pipe cleaners
- ribbon
- scissors
- glue
- paintbrushes
- pencil

Directions

1. Cut each egg cup to resemble a flower.
2. Paint each egg-cup flower the desired color.
3. After the paint dries, use the pencil to poke two small holes about ½-inch-apart in the bottom of each flower.
4. To make a stem, bend a pipe cleaner in half. Thread it through the holes in the bottom of the flower; then gently twist the ends together.
5. Glue a crumpled piece of tissue paper in the center of each flower.
6. To make a bouquet, tie the flower stems together with ribbon.

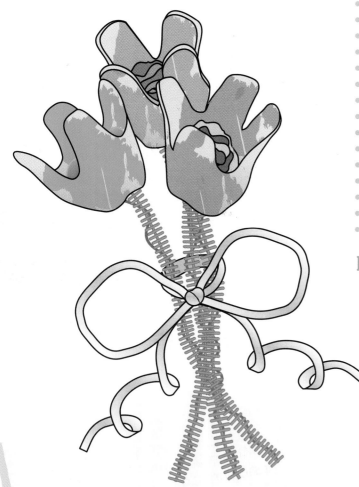

Teacher Tip

- If desired, cut out green construction paper leaves for each flower. Poke a hole in each leaf and then thread it onto the stem before twisting the pipe cleaners together. Then twist the stem together to hold the leaves in place.

Susan DeRiso—Barrington, RI

"Hand-some" Elephant

This cute elephant is a handful of fun to make. Line these unique creations up in parade fashion to give youngsters some counting practice. Or add them to your big-top display to enhance your circus unit.

Materials (per child)

- gray construction paper
- gray yarn
- small, dark fabric circle
- crayons or markers
- scissors
- glue
- clear tape

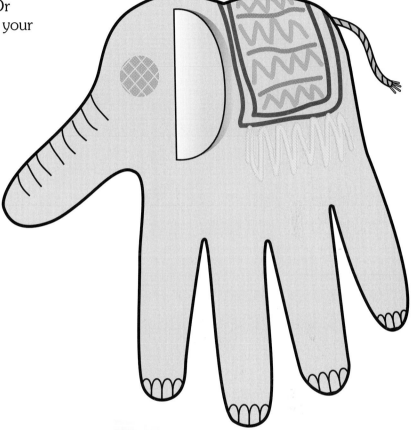

Directions

1. To make an elephant's body, spread out your thumb as far as possible (this will be the elephant's trunk). Trace your hand on gray paper; then cut out the outline.
2. Glue on a fabric eye.
3. Cut out a gray oval elephant ear. Fold the ear and glue it on the elephant.
4. Tape a yarn tail to the back of the elephant.
5. Draw additional details on the elephant as desired.

Teacher Tips

- As an alternative, have the child use gray paint to make a handprint on white paper for the elephant. Then have him cut out the shape and follow Steps 2–5 to decorate it.
- If desired, draw a decorative blanket on the elephant's back.

Linda Masternak Justice—Kansas City, MO

Star Clown

This delightful character will quickly become the star of your circus unit. Suspend these creative clowns from your ceiling for a show-stopping display.

Materials (per child)

tagboard clown body tracer (see Teacher Tips)
white construction paper clown face (see Teacher Tips)
colorful construction paper (including one large sheet)
paper-punch and die-cut shapes
    assorted craft items
    crayons or markers
    scissors
    glue

Directions

1. Outline the clown body tracer on colorful construction paper; then cut it out.
2. Cut out the clown face; then glue it on the body as shown.
3. Cut out hands and feet from your choice of paper colors. Glue them on the clown.
4. Draw details on the face.
5. Decorate the clown as desired.

Teacher Tips

● To make a tracer, cut out an enlarged tagboard copy of the clown body pattern (page 123).
● Enlarge the clown face pattern (page 123) by the same amount as the clown body so that they are proportionate. Then copy the face pattern on white construction paper.

Susan Bunyan—Dodge City, KS

Circus Clown Collar

Invite your little ones to clown around in these colorful clown collars. Divide your students into small groups; then encourage each group to make up its own clown act to perform for the class.

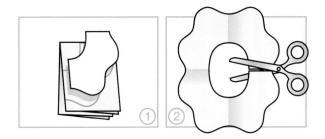

① ②

Materials (per child)

- tagboard clown collar tracer (see Teacher Tips)
- large sheet of colorful construction paper
- assorted craft items
- two 12" lengths of yarn
- scissors
- glue
- hole puncher
- pencil

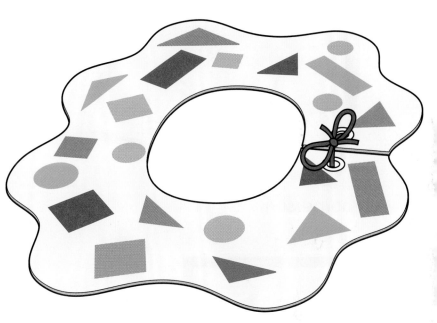

Directions

1. Fold the construction paper into fourths. Place the straight edges of the collar on the folds as shown. Trace the pattern; then cut it out through all thicknesses.
2. Unfold the collar. Cut along the fold on one of the narrower sides to create an opening.
3. Decorate the collar with the craft items of your choice.
4. Punch a hole in each end of the collar. Tie a length of yarn to each hole.

Teacher Tips
- To make a tracer, cut out a tagboard copy of the clown collar pattern on page 124.
- To increase durability, affix a hole reinforcer to each side of the tie holes before attaching the yarn.

Nancy Lotzer—Dallas, TX

Weather Wheel Patterns
Use with "Weather Wheel" on page 112.

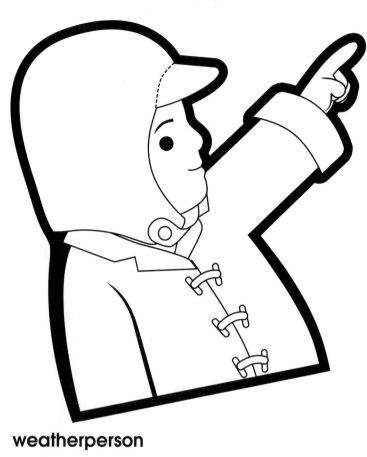

weather words

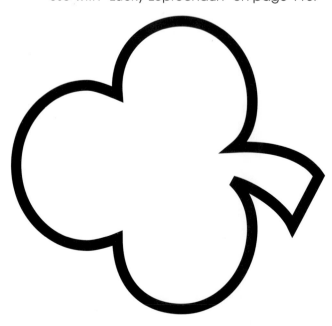

snowy

cloudy

sunny

rainy

weatherperson

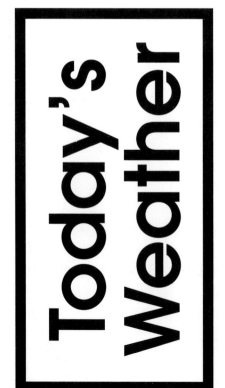

title

Shamrock Pattern
Use with "Lucky Leprechaun" on page 116.

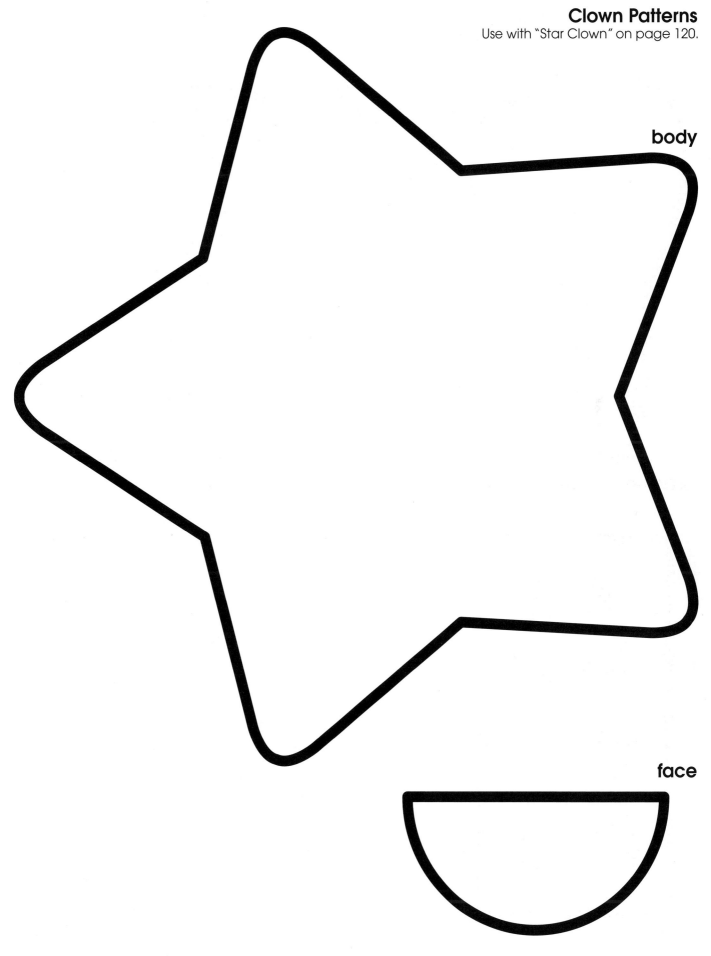

body

face

Clown Collar Pattern
Use with "Circus Clown Collar" on page 121.

Place on fold.

Place on fold.

APRIL

Nesting Hen

Mother Hen has a surprise in her nest! Use this clever project to enhance your spring studies.

Materials (per child)

- yellow construction paper copy of circle pattern (page 139)
- 6" paper plate
- 2 small black pom-poms
- orange construction paper scraps
- 2 or 3 yellow cotton balls
- brown crinkle strips
- brown tempera paint   glue
- paintbrush   fine-tipped
- scissors   black marker

Directions

1. Paint the plate brown and let it dry.
2. Cut out the yellow circle. Then cut out each wedge (in the circle) along the bold lines. Fringe-cut the wide, rounded end of each wedge.
3. Glue the straight edges of the circle section together to form a cone (the hen). While the glue is still wet, slide the point of one of the wedges between the glued edges to make a tail.
4. To make wings, glue the remaining two wedges on the hen.
5. Glue on the pom-pom eyes and an orange construction paper beak.
6. To create a nest, glue crinkle strips on the plate.
7. Glue the cotton balls (baby chicks) in the center of the nest. Add an orange beak to each chick; then use a fine-tipped black marker to dot on little eyes.
8. Set the hen on the nest so that it covers the chicks.

Teacher Tip
- If yellow cotton balls are not available, use yellow pom-poms for the chicks.

Margaret Southard—Cleveland, NY

Spring Basket

This adorable basket is easy to make and roomy enough for lots of seasonal goodies.

Materials (per child)

- tagboard fence tracer (see Teacher Tips)
- large paper grocery bag
- five 6" x 9" sheets of white construction paper
- assorted construction paper scraps
- scissors
- stapler
- glue

Directions

1. To make the basket, cut off the top half of the bag and set that part aside to use later for the handle.
2. Fold down the top edge of the bag about 1½ inches; then fold it down again.
3. To make a handle, cut the top portion of the bag open and cut a long three-inch-wide strip from it. Fold and glue the strip in thirds (lengthwise) and then in half as shown.
4. When the glue is dry, staple the handle to the bag.
5. To make the fence, fold each sheet of white paper in half twice and outline the tracer as indicated; then cut it out. *Do not cut the folded edges.*
6. Unfold the fence cutouts; then glue them around the basket. Trim off any excess paper.
7. Cut out stems, leaves, and flowers from construction paper. Then glue the cutouts to the basket, gluing some stems behind the fence and some in front of it.

Mary Maurer—Caddo, OK

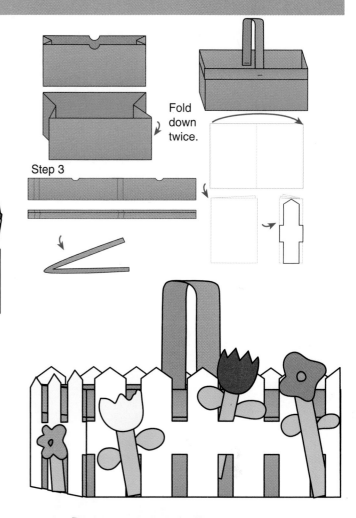

Fold down twice.

Step 3

Teacher Tips

- To make a tracer, cut out a tagboard copy of the fence pattern on page 139.
- If desired, line the basket with shredded paper or Easter grass.

Chick Mask

Here chicky, chicky, chicky! You'll hear happy peeps from your youngsters as they use these masks to role-play chick stories and songs.

Materials (per child)

- paper plate half
- orange construction paper
- two 12" lengths of yellow yarn
- yellow tempera paint
- several small feathers
- scissors
- paintbrush
- hole puncher
- glue

Directions

1. Paint the paper plate half yellow. Let the paint dry.
2. To make the mask, cut the rim off the plate as shown.
3. Cut out two eyeholes above the straight edge of the mask.
4. Cut out an orange triangle beak. Glue the beak and feathers to the mask. When the glue is dry, fold the beak up so that it points forward.
5. Punch a hole on each side of the mask as shown. (See Teacher Tip.)
6. Tie a length of yarn to each hole.

Teacher Tip
- If desired, back each hole with a hole reinforcer before tying the yarn to the mask.

Susan DeRiso—Barrington, RI

Sammy Salamander

These slim salamanders can hang onto clothing, fingers, and almost anything else they can get their hands on! Invite students to include their critters in their pretend pond play as well as in measurement activities.

Note: *This project is not waterproof and is not intended for water play.*

Materials (per child)

- 2 orange craft sticks (see Teacher Tips)
- 12" length of 3 mm orange pipe cleaner
- 2 small black pom-poms
- black permanent marker (fine-tipped)
- clothespins
- craft glue
- scissors
- pencil

Directions

1. Cut the pipe cleaner into the following lengths: one four-inch tail, two two-inch legs, and four one-inch feet.
2. To make each pair of legs, wrap a one-inch foot around each end of a two-inch leg (as shown). Then add a dot of glue to hold each piece in place.
3. Glue a leg section about one inch from each end of a craft stick. Then glue the four-inch tail on one end of the stick.
4. Glue the other craft stick on top of the legs and tail. Use clothespins to hold the sticks firmly together while the glue dries.
5. Use the marker to draw dots on the salamander.
6. Glue pom-pom eyes on the head and let the glue dry.
7. To curl the tail, wrap it around the pencil; then remove the pencil.

Mackie Rhodes—Greensboro, NC

Teacher Tips

- Color each craft stick with an orange marker. Spray the sticks with clear acrylic spray; then let them dry. This will keep the color from rubbing off on your fingers.
- Bend, twist, or wrap the tail to hang the salamander on objects.
- Blend in some phonics practice by encouraging each child to think of a name that begins with *S* for his salamander.

Pop Bottle Pig

These marvelous muddy pigs are the perfect addition to dramatic-play activities. And after that, encourage each child to use his pop bottle piggy to help him save his pennies at home.

Materials (per child)

- pink construction paper copy of pig ears patterns (page 142)
- tagboard pig foot tracer (see Teacher Tips)
- pink poster board
- lidded pop bottle
- pink glue paint (see Teacher Tips)
- brown tempera paint
- 6" length of pink pipe cleaner
- cotton balls
- scissors
- pencil
- craft glue
- craft knife
- paintbrush (for adult use)

Directions

1. To make the pig, remove the lid from the bottle. Paint the lid and bottle. *Do not paint the threads on the bottle.*
2. Tightly screw the lid on; then paint on brown eyes and nostrils. Use a cotton ball to lightly dab mud (brown paint) on the pig. Let the paint dry.
3. Outline the foot tracer four times on poster board. Cut out each foot; then also cut out the ears.
4. Glue the ears, feet, and pipe cleaner tail to the body.
5. After the glue dries, have an adult cut a slot in the top of the pig.
6. To curl the tail, wrap it around the pencil and then slide the pencil out.
7. To empty the bank, ask an adult to remove the snout and pour out the pennies.

Margaret Southard—Cleveland, NY

Teacher Tips

- Cut out tagboard copies of the pig feet (page 142) to use as tracers.
- To make the glue paint, mix equal amounts of pink tempera paint and glue; then stir in a few drops of dishwashing liquid (this will help the paint adhere to the plastic bottle).

Tissue Paper Bird

Youngsters will have lots to chirp about when you fill your classroom with these unique and colorful birds.

Materials (per child)

- paper plate
- tissue paper in assorted colors
- orange and white construction paper
- water-thinned glue
- black marker
- scissors
- paintbrush
- glue
- hole puncher
- yarn
- stapler

Directions

1. Cut your color choice(s) of tissue paper into small squares.
2. Fold the plate in half.
3. Open the plate and paint the entire back of the plate with water-thinned glue. Then press tissue paper squares on the glue.
4. Refold the plate.
5. Cut out four 2" x 6" tissue paper strips to use for tail feathers. Staple them to one end of the bird as shown.
6. Cut out white circles for eyes. Use the marker to draw the pupil on each eye. Glue an eye on each side of the bird.
7. Cut out an orange triangle beak. Fold the beak in half; then glue it inside the fold of the bird as shown. Let the glue dry.
8. To display the bird, punch a hole in the top (through both thicknesses) and tie on a yarn hanger.

Susan DeRiso—Barrington, RI

Teacher Tip

- If desired, skip Step 8 and let the birds rest on tables and countertops in your classroom.

Dandy Dragonfly

What's all the buzz about? These unique child-made insects! Add these dragonflies to your dramatic-play center to prompt some pond-life role-playing.

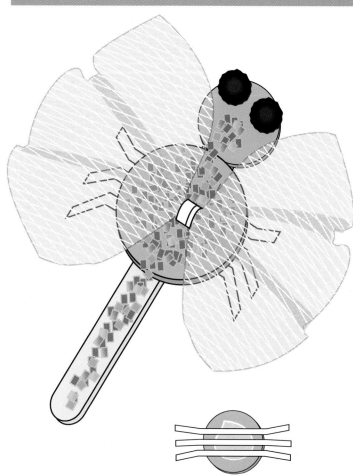

Materials (per child)

- 4" square of white tulle (see Teacher Tip)
- 1" blue craft foam circle
- 2" blue craft foam circle
- craft stick
- 4 twist ties
- 2 small black pom-poms
- blue and green glitter
- scissors
- craft glue
- clothespin
- pencil

Directions

1. To make a body with legs, glue three twist ties across the large circle as shown.
2. Glue the small circle (head) on the end of the craft stick. Then glue the body next to it. Use a clothespin to hold the body in place while the glue dries.
3. Glue a mixture of blue and green glitter on the head, body, and exposed craft stick. Then glue the pom-pom eyes on the head.
4. Cut the last twist tie in half. Wrap one of the halves around the middle of the tulle square to make wings. Glue the wings to the body.
5. After the glue dries, fluff the wings and shape the legs.

Teacher Tip
- Tulle is a fine netting used in bridal veils and dance costumes. It is available in fabric and craft stores.

Julie Koczur

Bunny Planter

Celebrate Earth Day by planting flower seeds in this earth-friendly bunny planter. Then encourage youngsters to nurture their seeds from sprouts to blooms. Hop to it!

Materials (per child)

- plastic laundry scoop
- 2 wooden craft spoons (ears)
- 2 tiny black pom-poms (eyes)
- small black pom-pom (nose)
- 5 brown pom-poms (feet and tail)
- brown glue paint (see Teacher Tips)
- black permanent marker
- craft glue
- paintbrush
- soil
- marigold seeds (or other flower seeds with a short germination period)

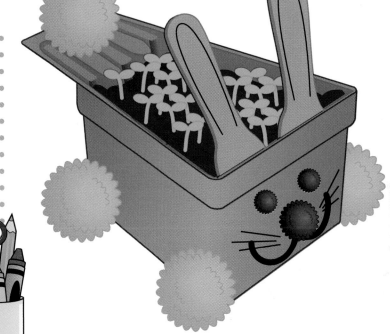

Directions

1. Paint one side of each craft spoon (ear). Then paint the sides and handle of the laundry scoop. Let the paint dry.
2. Glue the wide end of each ear to the inside of the laundry scoop (planter).
3. Glue pom-pom eyes and a nose on the flat side of the planter.
4. Glue a pom-pom tail on the handle; then glue two pom-pom feet on each side of the planter.
5. After the glue dries, use the marker to draw whiskers, a mouth, and other details.
6. Fill the planter with soil; then plant a few seeds in it.

Teacher Tips

- To make glue paint, mix equal amounts of glue and brown paint. Then add a few drops of dishwashing liquid (this helps the paint adhere to the plastic).
- Use clothespins to hold the ears in place while the glue dries.

Mackie Rhodes—Greensboro, NC

Rain Cloud

It's raining! It's pouring! Youngsters will enjoy pretty indoor rain showers when you display these rain mobiles in your classroom.

Materials (per child)

- 9" paper plate
- cotton balls
- 4" square of blue copy paper
- white thread
- ribbon
- scissors
- clear tape
- hole puncher
- glue

Directions

1. Cut out a cloud shape from the paper plate. Glue cotton balls on the cutout.
2. For each raindrop, fold a square of copy paper in half and then in half again to create a smaller square.
3. Cut out a raindrop from the smaller square.
4. Using tape and thread, suspend each raindrop from the cloud.
5. Punch two holes in the top of the cloud. Tie a length of ribbon to the cloud to create a hanger.

Teacher Tip

- To make the cloud less bulky (and use fewer cotton balls), stretch out the cotton balls before gluing them on the cloud.

Susan DeRiso—Barrington, RI

Bubbly Umbrella

Invite youngsters to create designer umbrellas with this bubble activity. Display the completed projects in a window or on a light blue background.

Materials (per child)

- tagboard umbrella and handle tracers (see Teacher Tips)
- corn syrup bubble solution (see Teacher Tips)
- plastic nut cup for each color of bubble solution
- colorful construction paper
- clear report cover   pencil
- drinking straw   waxed paper
- scissors   tape

Directions

1. Cut off the fold and the holes of the report cover. Place one sheet on waxed paper.
2. While holding the cup above the clear sheet, put the straw in it and blow until bubbles flow onto the sheet.
3. Repeat Step 2 for each desired color.
4. Let the bubbles dry for a day or two. (Most of the bubbles will pop.)
5. When the design is tacky to the touch—but not runny—firmly press the other clear sheet on top of it. Let it dry for one to two more days.
6. Fold the construction paper in half. Place the straight edges of the umbrella tracer on the fold. Outline the tracer and then cut it out.
7. Outline the handle tracer and cut it out.
8. Use rolled tape to back the umbrella cutout with the bubble design. Trim off the excess; then tape the handle to the umbrella.

Mackie Rhodes—Greensboro, NC

Teacher Tips

- To make tracers, cut out a tagboard copy of the umbrella and handle patterns (page 140).
- For each color of bubble solution, mix two tablespoons light corn syrup and a half teaspoon water in a plastic nut cup. Add a drop of food coloring and a few drops of dishwashing liquid.
- To help keep the child from sucking the bubble solution into his mouth, use a pushpin to poke a small hole near the top of the straw.

Lovely Lily Pad

Convert a simple paper plate into a pretty lily pad!

Materials (per child)

- 9" paper plate
- 2½" cupcake liner
- 2" cupcake liner (mini size)
- two 2½" lengths of yellow pipe cleaner
- green tempera paint
- scissors
- glue
- paintbrush

Directions

1. Paint the front and back of the paper plate green. Let the paint dry.
2. Cut one side of the plate to resemble a lily pad.
3. To make a flower, cut slits around the edge of the large cupcake liner as shown. Glue the small cupcake liner to the center of the large one; then glue the flower to the lily pad.
4. Twist the pipe cleaners together; then glue them to the center of the flower.
5. When the glue is dry, spread out the flower petals and shape the pipe cleaners.

Teacher Tip

- Use the lily pad as a math mat and have each child count out designated numbers of toy frogs onto his lily pad. Or have him use the frogs and his lily pad to practice positional concepts such as in, on, under, and around.

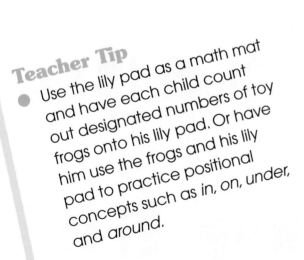

adapted from ideas by
Julie Koczur and Susan DeRiso—Barrington, RI

Hoppin' Frog Puppet

Youngsters will hop right into some "ribbeting" role-playing with these little green critters.

Materials (per child)

- green construction paper copy of frog legs and arms pattern (page 141)
- three 9" paper plates
- 2 milk jug lids
- white construction paper
- 5" length of red curling ribbon
- red and green tempera paint
- black marker
- scissors
- glue
- paintbrushes
- clothespins

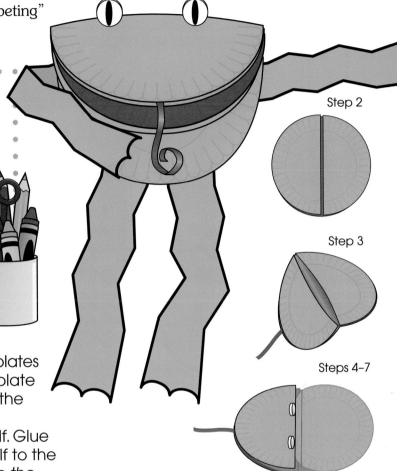

Step 2

Step 3

Steps 4–7

Directions

1. Paint the fronts and backs of two plates green. Paint one side of the third plate green and the other side red. Let the paint dry.
2. Cut one of the green plates in half. Glue just the curved edges of each half to the back of the red plate. *Do not glue the straight edges.*
3. While the glue is still wet, trap one end of the ribbon between the two plates.
4. Fold the red plate with the red inside.
5. Fold down one-fourth of the remaining green plate. Glue that flap inside the bottom of the mouth.
6. To make eyes, trace each jug lid on white paper. Cut out each circle, draw on a pupil, and glue it to a lid.
7. Glue on each eye as shown. (See Teacher Tips.)
8. Cut out the legs and arms. Accordion-fold each one; then glue it to the back of the frog's body.
9. When the glue is dry, curl the frog's tongue.

Julie Koczur

Teacher Tips

- Use clothespins to hold pieces together while the glue dries.
- If milk jug lids are not available, simply cut out large white construction paper eyes, draw on pupils, and then glue a small folded-back section to the frog.

Watercolor Wonders

These pictures are simple to make and simply beautiful! Use them to adorn your classroom walls, windows, or even the hallway.

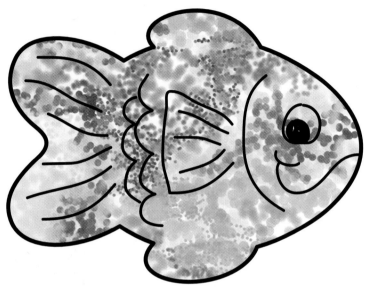

Materials (per child)

- newspaper
- sheet of white construction paper
- white construction paper shape of your choice (see Teacher Tip)
- water-based markers
- spray bottle filled with water
- scissors (optional)

Directions

1. Set the white paper on several layers of newspaper.
2. Use markers to draw a variety of designs—such as dots, curves, and shapes—on the white paper.
3. Lightly spray water on the marker designs. (Observe how the colors bleed and blend into each other.)
4. Gently press the white shape on the wet design; then lift it off and let it dry.
5. Add details with a marker.
6. If desired, cut out a different shape from the original paper.

Teacher Tip
- To make the shape shown, use the pattern on page 142.

Linda Rasmussen—Reno, NV

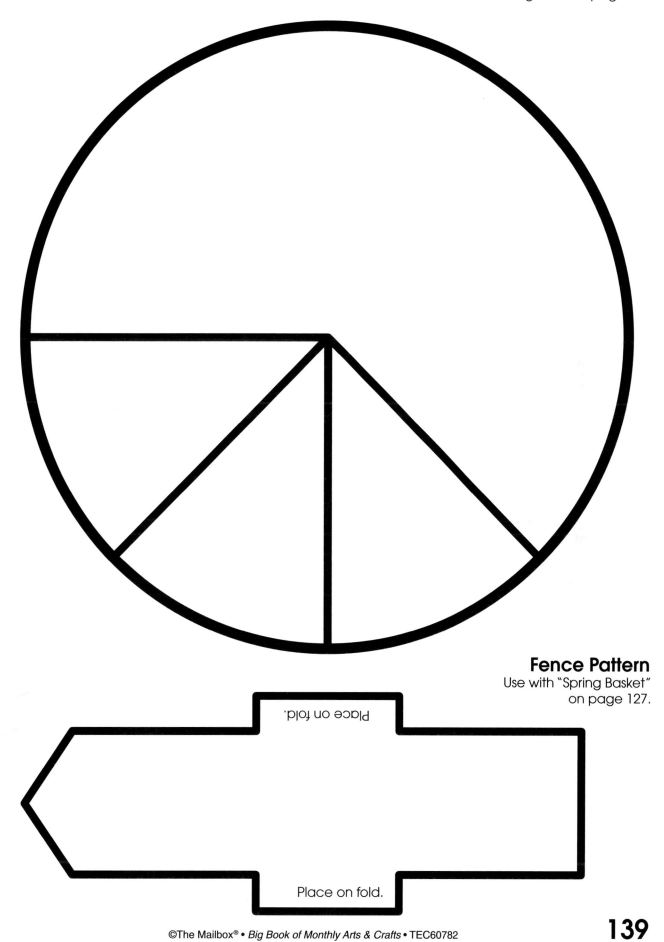

Fence Pattern
Use with "Spring Basket"
on page 127.

Place on fold.

Place on fold.

Umbrella and Handle Patterns
Use with "Bubbly Umbrella" on page 135.

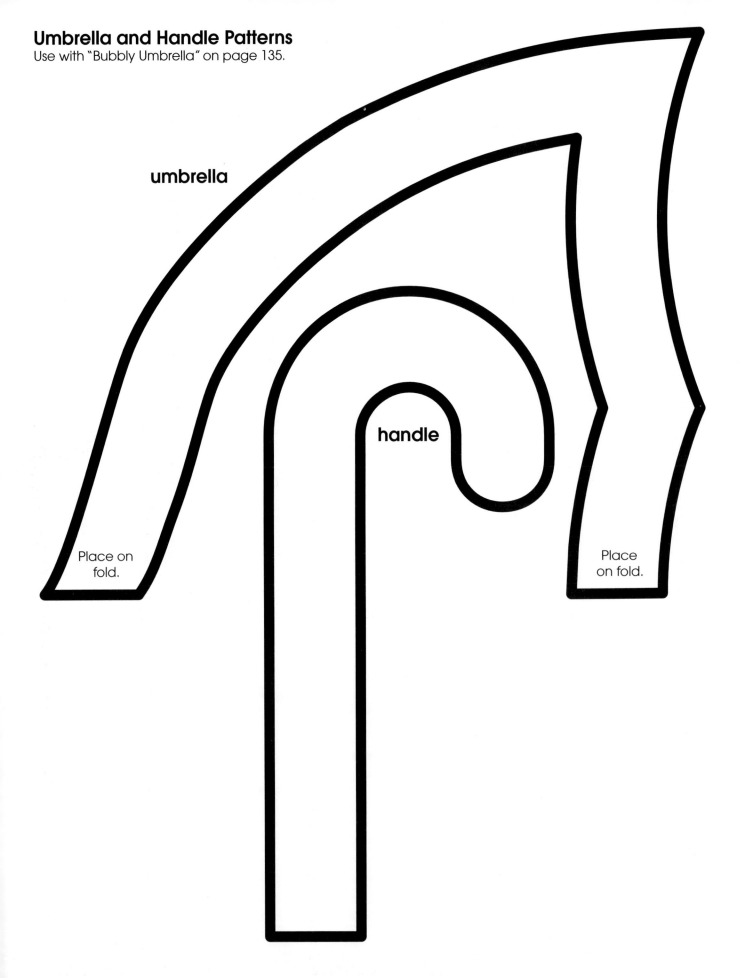

umbrella

handle

Place on fold.

Place on fold.

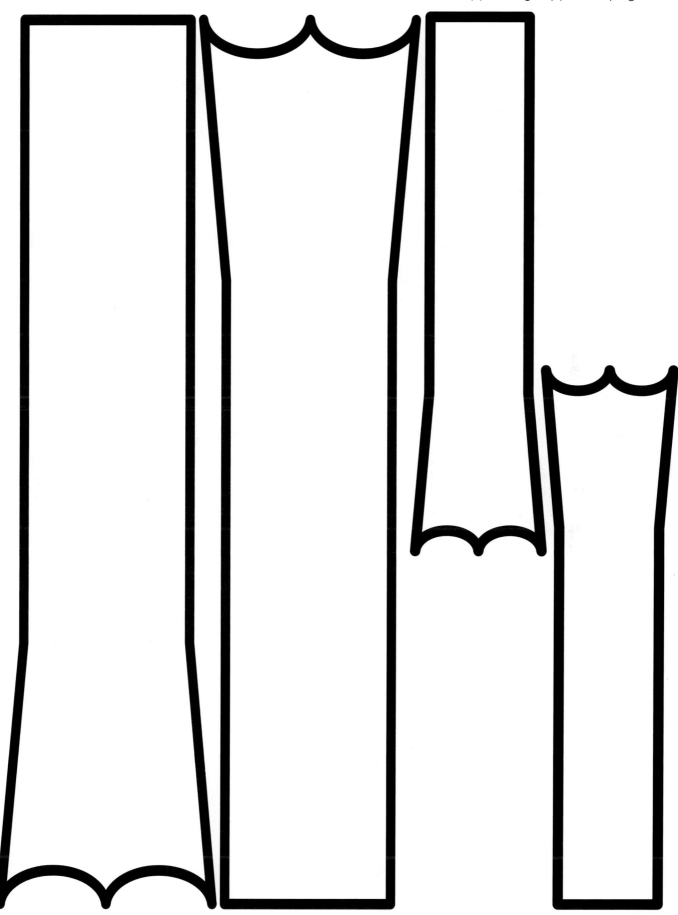

Pig Patterns
Use with "Pop Bottle Pig" on page 130.

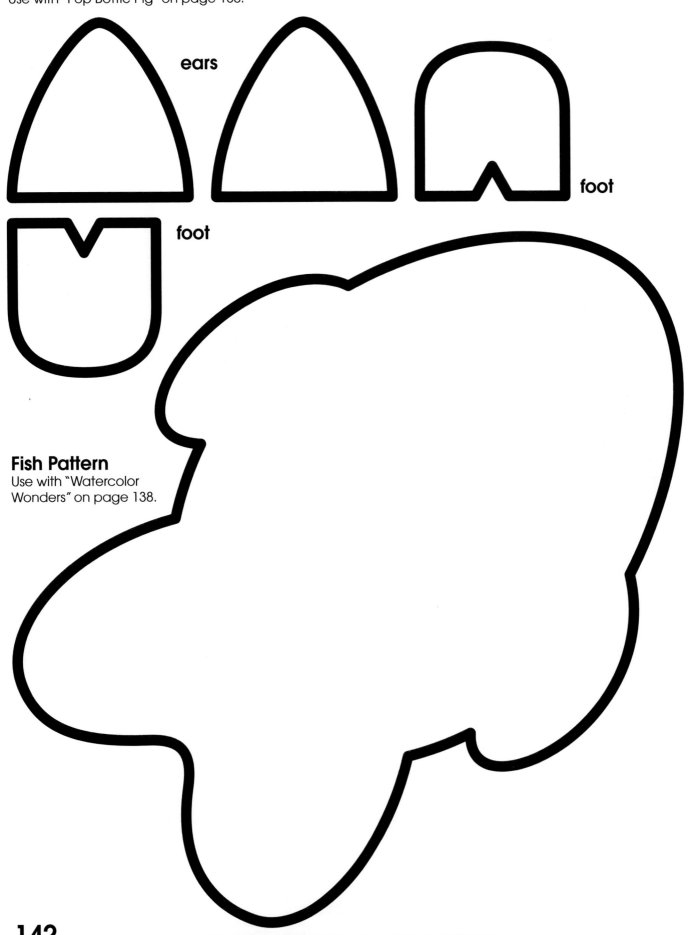

ears

foot

foot

Fish Pattern
Use with "Watercolor Wonders" on page 138.

MAY

Recipe Card Holder

Clip each child's special Mother's Day message to this unique flower. Then have the child give her flower to her mother to use as a holder for recipes or notes.

I love you Mom

Steps 2 and 3

Materials (per child)

- tagboard flower tracer (see Teacher Tips)
- colorful 5" poster board square
- 8-oz. foam cup
- 9" length of 18-gauge floral wire (wrapped)
- clothespin
- tissue paper scraps
- small tissue paper squares
- water-thinned glue (see Teacher Tips)
- brown glue (see Teacher Tips)
- rice
- crayons
- scissors
- pencil
- paintbrush
- hot glue (for adult use)

Directions

1. Trace the flower onto the poster board and then cut it out. Glue a scrunched-up tissue paper center in the middle.
2. Slip one end of the wire through the spring on the clothespin; then bend it across the clothespin as shown.
3. Have an adult hot-glue the clothespin to the back of the flower.
4. Use the water-thinned glue to paint tissue paper squares all over the cup.
5. Fill the cup with rice.
6. Poke the stem into the rice so that it stands upright; then cover the rice with a thin layer of brown glue. Let the glue dry.
7. To make leaves, tie a green tissue paper square around the stem; then glue it in place.

Elizabeth Trautman—Greensboro, NC

Teacher Tips

- To make a tracer, cut out a tagboard copy of the flower pattern on page 157.
- To make water-thinned glue, mix equal parts of white glue with water.
- To make brown glue, mix a few drops of brown paint into white glue.
- If desired, complete Steps 1–3 for your students in advance.

Letter-Perfect Picture Frame

Youngsters are sure to capture the hearts of their loved ones with these letter-perfect frames.

Materials (per child)

- tagboard copy of the picture frame pattern (page 156)
- photo of child (to fit opening of frame)
- watercolor paints
- paintbrush
- Alpha-Bits cereal (see Teacher Tips)
- scissors
- glue

Directions

1. Cut out the picture frame; then cut out the heart-shaped opening.
2. Paint the frame with a coat of water-color paint and let it dry.
3. Glue the photo to the back of the opening.
4. Fold the frame in half as shown. Glue cereal letters on the frame to spell a message or a name, or just to create a design.
5. When the glue is dry, cut along the dotted lines on the back of the frame to create a stand. Fold the stand up and away from the frame.
6. Glue the back and front of the frame together. *Do not glue the stand.*
7. After the glue dries, stand the picture upright on a flat surface.

Teacher Tips

- To preserve the cereal glued to the frame, lightly brush white glue over each piece. Let the cereal dry.
- For added stability, fold over one-quarter inch of the bottom of the stand.

Cynthia Holzschuher—Lebanon, OH

Handmade Lily

Youngsters will be proud to hand this one-of-a-kind lily to a special friend or family member. You might even invite each child to make several lilies to present in a bouquet to his loved one.

Materials (per child)

- white and green construction paper
- long green pipe cleaner
- 6" yellow pipe cleaner
- watercolor paint   paintbrush
- scissors   pencil
- clothespin   glue

Directions

1. Trace your hand on white construction paper; then cut out the outline.
2. Paint the hand cutout; then let it dry.
3. Glue the palm end of the hand into a cone shape as shown, leaving a small opening at the bottom.
4. Fold the yellow pipe cleaner in half. Starting at the fold, twist about half of the pipe cleaner together. Then bend and shape the three ends to resemble the center of a flower.
5. Wrap one end of the green pipe cleaner around the middle of the yellow flower center.
6. Slide the loose end of the green pipe cleaner through the opening in the lily. Add a dot of glue to hold the flower in place.
7. Cut out and glue construction paper leaves to the stem, using a clothespin to hold them in place while the glue dries.
8. To curl the flower, roll the finger petals around a pencil and then release them.

Jana Sanderson—Stockton, CA

Step 3

Step 4

Step 5

Teacher Tip

- If needed, use a clothespin to hold the hand in a cone shape while the glue dries.

Fuzzy Caterpillar

Invite youngsters to make these fuzzy, curvy creatures to enhance your science studies. Display the caterpillars on a spring scene or use them as a border for a spring display.

Materials (per child)

- construction paper copy of the caterpillar pattern (page 157)
- short lengths of thick yarn (to match caterpillar color)
- white hole reinforcer
- glue
- scissors

Directions

1. Cut out the caterpillar.
2. Stretch out the individual strands in each yarn length. Then glue the fuzzy pieces of yarn to the caterpillar.
3. Stick on the white hole-reinforcer eye.

Teacher Tip

● If desired, use different yarn colors to create stripes or other designs on the caterpillar.

Jana Sanderson—Stockton, CA

Butterfly Light Catcher

These butterflies will create a flutter of compliments when you display them in your classroom windows.

Materials (per child)

- tagboard butterfly tracer (see Teacher Tips)
- 12" x 14" sheet of waxed paper
- 12" x 18" sheet of black construction paper
- white crayon (or chalk)
- two tiny black pom-poms
- assorted tissue paper
- multicolored glitter
- pipe cleaner
- paintbrush
- scissors
- glue
- pushpin
- tape
- pencil

Directions

1. Fold the black paper in half. Place the straight edge of the tracer along the fold; then trace it.
2. Cut out the shape (including the wing openings); then unfold it and glue it to the waxed paper.
3. Paint each wing opening with glue; then cover it with small tissue paper pieces. Paint on another coat of glue; then let it dry.
4. Glue pom-pom eyes on the butterfly. Then use glue to draw on a mouth and other details. Sprinkle glitter on the glue and let it dry.
5. Trim the waxed paper to the shape of the butterfly.
6. Use a pushpin to poke two holes in the head. Then, from the back of the head, push each end of the pipe cleaner through a different hole to create antennae.
7. To curl the antennae, wrap each one around a pencil.

Susan DeRiso—Barrington, RI

Teacher Tip
- To make a tracer, cut out a tagboard copy of the butterfly pattern on page 158. Cut out the wing openings where indicated.
- Add a small amount of water to the glue so that it spreads easily.
- To stabilize the antennae, tape them to the back of the butterfly's head.

Picnic Basket

A tisket, a tasket, what a precious picnic basket! Invite youngsters to take their personal picnic baskets outdoors to enjoy a class picnic.

Materials (per child)

- brown paper lunch bag
- 1½" x 18" brown construction paper strip
- white paper towel (high quality works best)
- two 1" sponge squares
- brown and red tempera paint
- stapler
- picnic supplies (such as a 6" paper plate, an 8-oz. foam cup, plastic utensils, and a napkin)

Directions

1. To make the basket, fold down a one-inch cuff around the top of the bag. Fold the cuff down four more times so that the bag stands about four to five inches tall.
2. Sponge-paint a brown checkerboard pattern on the basket. Let the paint dry.
3. Staple the brown paper strip to the basket to create a handle as shown.
4. Sponge-paint a red checkerboard pattern on the paper towel. Let the paint dry.
5. Line the basket with the paper towel; then pack it with the picnic items.

Step 1

Teacher Tip

- If desired, ask parent volunteers to prefold the paper bag baskets for your class.

Susan DeRiso—Barrington, RI

Strawberry Glasses

It's a strawberry world when youngsters peer through these special glasses.

Materials (per child)

tagboard strawberry glasses and cap
    tracers (see Teacher Tips)
red and green craft foam
two 8" lengths of red pipe
    cleaner
gold paint pen
craft glue
scissors
pushpin
pencil

Directions

1. Trace the glasses on red craft foam and the strawberry cap twice on green craft foam. Cut out all the patterns.
2. Use the gold paint pen to dot seeds on the glasses.
3. Glue the strawberry caps to the glasses as shown. Let the glue dry.
4. Use a pushpin to poke a hole near each top corner of the glasses. Carefully push the end of a pipe cleaner through each hole; then twist it to secure it in place.
5. Put on the glasses; then bend the earpieces to fit your head.

Teacher Tips
- To make tracers, cut out a tagboard copy of the glasses and strawberry cap patterns on page 159.
- If desired, have adult volunteers cut out a class supply of glasses in advance.
- Bend the tip of each earpiece back on itself to avoid scratching.

Susan DeRiso—Barrington, RI

Strawberry Bell

For music time, dinnertime, or any old time, these little berry bells are nice to have on hand. Invite youngsters to play their bells during music activities at school. Later, encourage them to use them as dinner bells or musical door hangers at home.

Materials (per child)

- tagboard strawberry cap tracer (see Teacher Tips)
- green craft foam
- 1½" terra-cotta pot
- large jingle bell
- hole puncher
- 12" length of green ribbon
- red tempera paint
- black permanent marker
- scissors
- stapler
- craft glue
- paintbrush

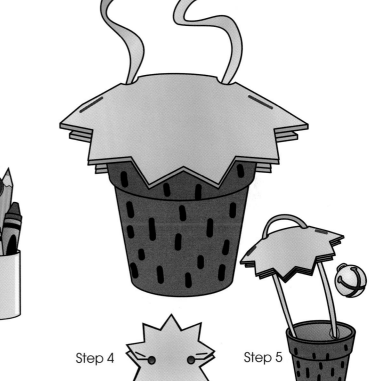

Step 4

Step 5

Directions

1. To make the strawberry, turn the pot upside down; then paint it red.
2. When the paint is dry, use the marker to dot seeds on the strawberry.
3. Trace the strawberry cap onto the craft foam; then mark the holes. Cut out the outline, punch out each hole, and then cut a slit on each side leading to the hole.
4. To contour the cap, overlap and staple each set of snipped ends together as shown.
5. Thread each end of the ribbon through a hole in the cap. Then glue the ribbon ends inside the strawberry as shown. Let the glue dry.
6. Place the bell inside the strawberry; then line the rim with glue. Slide the cap down the ribbon and press it firmly onto the strawberry. Let the glue dry.

Mackie Rhodes—Greensboro, NC

Teacher Tips

- To make a tracer, cut out a tagboard copy of the strawberry cap pattern on page 157. Punch out the holes where indicated.
- Use clothespins to hold the ribbon ends inside the strawberry while the glue dries.

"Bumble-Bag" Buddy

Youngsters will be delighted to include these little bumble buddies in their dramatic-play activities or related songs.

Step 3

Materials (per child)

- tagboard wing tracer (see Teacher Tips)
- paper lunch bag
- black construction paper
- 2 small black pom-poms (eyes)
- white chalk
- yellow and black tempera paint
- 6" black pipe cleaner
- pushpin
- newspaper
- permanent marker
- paintbrushes
- scissors
- tape
- stapler
- glue

Directions

1. Paint the bag yellow. Let the paint dry; then paint black stripes around the bag.
2. After the paint dries, use a pushpin to poke two holes in the bag where the antennae are.
3. Bend the pipe cleaner (as shown); then, from the inside of the bag, push each end of the pipe cleaner through a hole to make the antennae. Tape the pipe cleaner in place inside the bag.
4. Fill the bag with crumpled newspaper. Then fold the bag opening in a V shape. Staple the folded ends together.
5. Use the chalk to outline the wing twice on black paper. Cut out each wing and then fold down the square end.
6. Glue a wing to each side of the bag. Then glue on the pom-pom eyes.
7. After the glue dries, shape the antennae; then draw on additional features with the marker.

Susan DeRiso—Barrington, RI

Teacher Tips
- To make a tracer, cut out a tagboard copy of the wing pattern on page 159.
- If needed, use tape to hold the wings in place while the glue dries.

Sandy Seashell

Youngsters will think of lots of uses for this giant seashore treasure. To reinforce language skills, simply invite each child to hide an object under her seashell. Then have her give clues until a classmate guesses what's under the shell. Surprise!

Materials (per child)

- 9" paper plate
- tagboard shell base (see Teacher Tips)
- tempera paint in shell colors
- pale yellow glue paint (see Teacher Tips)
- sand
- iridescent glitter
- scissors
- paintbrush
- glue
- 2 clothespins

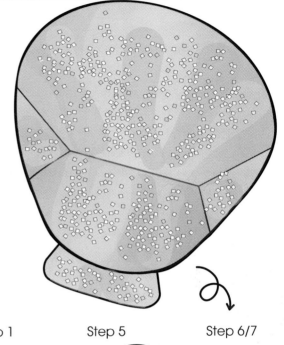

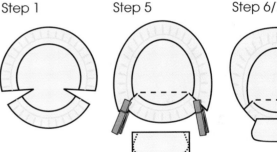

Step 1   Step 5   Step 6/7

Directions

1. Paint both sides of the plate and the shell base a shell color. Let the paint dry.
2. Mix a small amount of glitter with the sand.
3. Paint yellow streaks on the back of the plate; then sprinkle the sand mixture on the wet paint.
4. After the paint dries, cut out two wedges from the plate as shown.
5. To make a shell, overlap and glue the edges of each opening together. Use clothespins to hold the edges in place while the glue dries.
6. Glue the shell base to the plate rim as shown. Let the glue dry.
7. Trim the uneven edges of the shell.

Teacher Tips

- To make a shell base, cut out a 2" x 5" piece of tagboard. Trim the short sides according to the diagram.
- Mix yellow paint and white glue to make a pale yellow glue paint.
- If desired, make two shells; then staple their bases together to create a hinged shell.

Mackie Rhodes—Greensboro, NC

Under-the-Sea Scene

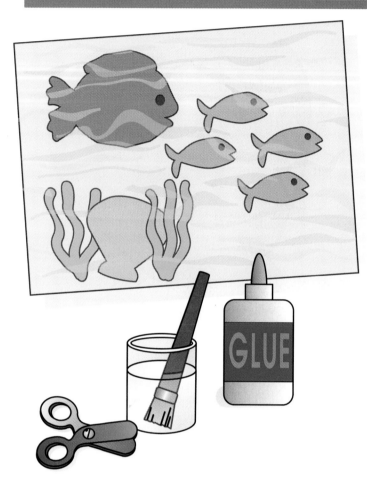

What's below the surface of the sea? Encourage youngsters to create what they imagine is there with these pretty underwater scenes. Display the completed projects on a dark blue background or in a classroom window.

Materials (per child)

- 12" x 18" sheet of white construction paper
- assorted colorful construction paper
- light blue tissue paper
- water-thinned glue
- paintbrush
- scissors
- pencil
- glue

Directions

1. Draw an assortment of sea life on a variety of colorful construction paper. Then cut out each drawing.
2. Glue the cutouts on the white paper to create a scene.
3. Paint the scene with water-thinned glue; then cover the picture with the light blue tissue paper. Let the glue dry.
4. Trim the tissue paper to the size of the scene.

Teacher Tip

- If desired, draw and cut out tagboard tracers of a variety of sea shapes. Then invite students to trace their choice of these shapes on construction paper.

Margaret Southard—Cleveland, NY

Safari Puppet Pals

Enhance your zoo unit with these adorable puppets.

Materials (per child)

- tagboard animal tracers (see Teacher Tips)
- one 8-oz. foam cup for each animal
- white construction paper (zebra)
- black tempera paint (zebra)
- yellow construction paper (giraffe)
- brown tempera paint (giraffe)
- yellow crayon (giraffe)
- 2 small black pom-poms for each animal
- pink construction paper scraps
- black permanent marker
- scissors, paintbrush, and glue
- pencil

Directions

1. For each animal, fold the appropriate color of construction paper in half. Place the straight edge of the tracer on the fold. Trace, cut out, and then unfold the shape.
2. For the giraffe, color the bottom and the lower half of the cup yellow. Print brown fingertip spots on the colored part of the cup and on the giraffe cutout.
3. For the zebra, paint a child's fingers black; then wrap them around the bottom half of the cup to create stripes. Make black fingerprint stripes on the zebra cutout.
4. After the paint dries, glue pom-pom eyes on each animal. Cut out four identical pink shapes; then glue them to the ears.
5. To complete each animal, slide the bottom of the cup through the hole. Use the marker to draw nostrils and a mouth on the cup bottom. Add other details as desired.

Mackie Rhodes—Greensboro, NC

Teacher Tips

- To make tracers, cut out tagboard copies of the puppet patterns on page 160.
- Depending on your students' abilities, you might prefer to have adult volunteers cut out the puppet patterns in advance.
- If desired, secure the animal cutout to the cup with tape.

155

Picture Frame Pattern

Use with "Letter-Perfect Picture Frame" on page 145.

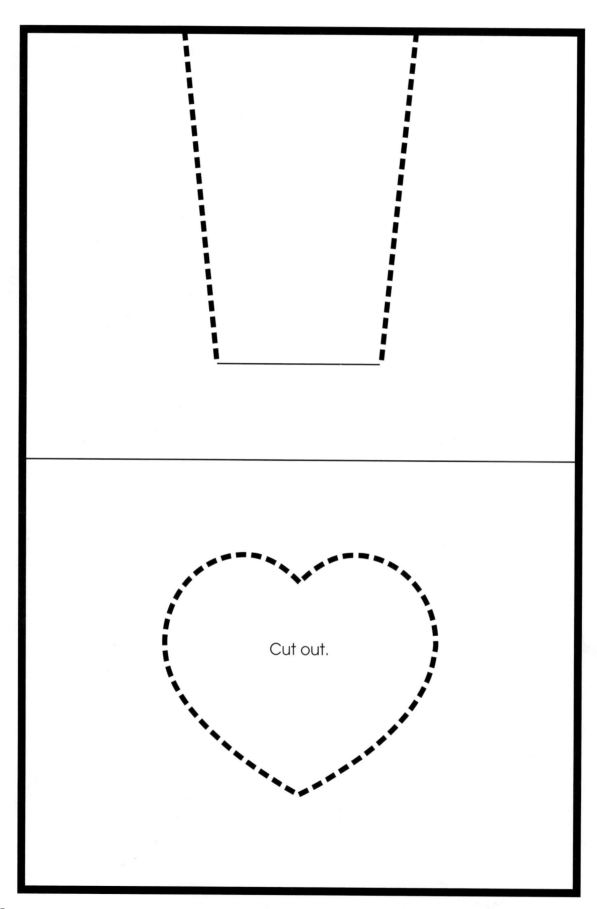

Cut out.

Caterpillar Pattern
Use with "Fuzzy Caterpillar" on page 147.

Strawberry Cap Pattern
Use with "Strawberry Bell" on page 151.

Flower Pattern
Use with "Recipe Card Holder" on page 144.

Butterfly Pattern

Use with "Butterfly Light Catcher" on page 148.

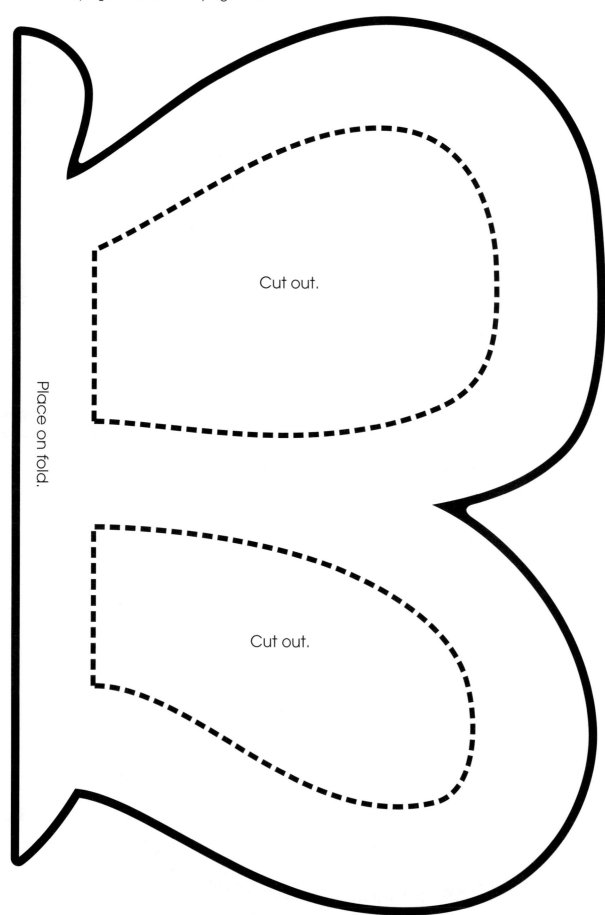

Cut out.

Place on fold.

Cut out.

Glasses and Strawberry Cap Patterns
Use with "Strawberry Glasses" on page 150.

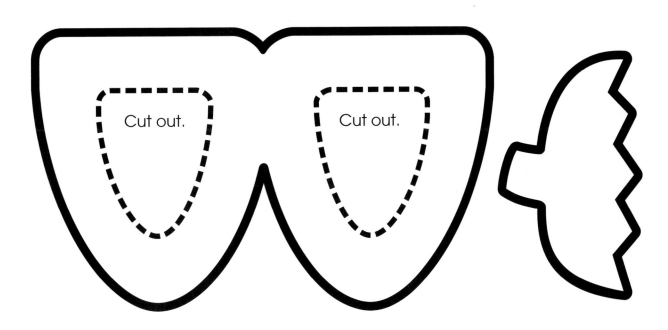

Cut out.

Cut out.

Wing Pattern
Use with "'Bumble-Bag' Buddy" on page 152.

Puppet Patterns
Use with "Safari Puppet Pals" on page 155.

zebra

giraffe

Place on fold.

Place on fold.

SUMMER

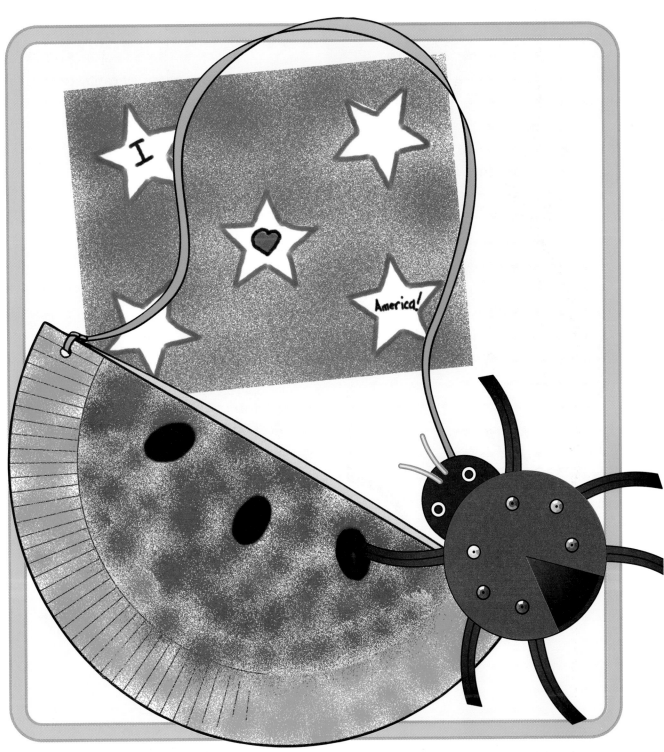

Rainbow Trout

From red to purple and green to yellow, this rainbow trout is a colorful fellow! Display these fish on your bulletin board so that they form a rainbow shape over a wavy line of blue water.

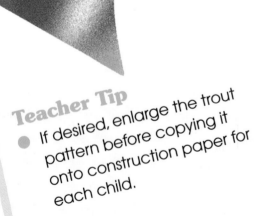

Materials (per child)

- construction paper copy of trout pattern (page 175)
- white hole reinforcer
- assorted paint colors (including black)
- medicine dropper for each paint color
- paint roller
- scissors
- glue

Directions

1. Cut out the trout pattern.
2. Use the medicine droppers to squeeze different-colored drops of paint all over the cutout.
3. Lightly coat the paint roller with your choice of one paint color. Then roll it over the cutout, spreading the drops of paint as you work.
4. When the colored paint dries, use black paint to make fingerprint spots along the top part of the trout.
5. Stick on the hole-reinforcer eye.

Teacher Tip
- If desired, enlarge the trout pattern before copying it onto construction paper for each child.

Jana Sanderson—Stockton, CA

Watermelon Holder

Who knows what kinds of collectibles your little ones will store in these keepsake holders! Invite each child to display his project on a doorknob at home and use it to store special summer mementos such as notes, photos, postcards, and shells.

Materials (per child)

- 9" paper plate
- red, green, and black tempera paint
- sponge
- ribbon
- scissors
- glue
- hole puncher

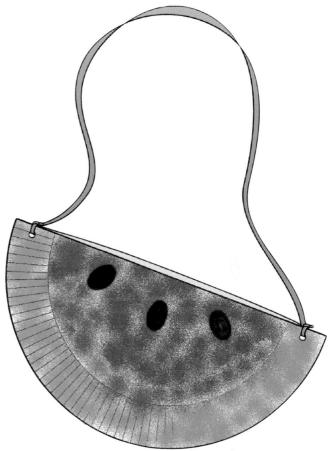

Directions

1. Turn the plate upside down; then sponge-paint the center part red. When the red paint dries, sponge-paint the edge of the plate green and let that paint dry.
2. Cut the plate in half to make two watermelon slices. Then print black fingerprint seeds on each slice. Let the paint dry.
3. Glue (or staple) together the curved edges of the two slices to create a pocket. Be sure to leave the straight edges open.
4. When the glue is dry, punch a hole near each corner of the watermelon slice. Make a hanger by tying each end of a length of ribbon to a hole.

Teacher Tips

- Use clothespins to hold the watermelon slices together while the glue dries.
- If desired, fill each child's project with end-of-the-year party favors. Encourage him to empty his holder at home and then use it as a family memento holder.

Susan DeRiso—Barrington, RI

Wandering Ladybug

Youngsters will get a kick out of hanging around with these larger-than-life ladybugs. Invite each child to bend and hook his ladybug's legs to attach it to a variety of objects.

Materials (per child)

- juice can lid
- 12 twist-ties, connected in sets of two
- 2 white hole-reinforcer eyes
- black craft foam circle (the size of a milk jug lid)
- 4" length of gold cord (or pipe cleaner)
- tiny sequins
- red felt
- black glue-paint (see Teacher Tips)
- scissors
- black marker (for tracing)
- craft glue
- paintbrush

Directions

1. Trace the juice can lid onto the red felt. Cut out the resulting circle; then cut out a small wedge from that circle.
2. Paint the underside of the lid with black glue-paint. Also paint one side of each set of twist-ties. Let all the paint dry.
3. Glue on the foam circle (head) and twist-tie legs as shown.
4. Glue the red wings onto the lid with the wedge opposite the head.
5. Cut the gold cord in half; then glue the pieces onto the head to resemble antennae.
6. Stick on hole-reinforcer eyes.
7. Glue tiny sequins onto the wings.
8. When the glue is dry, shape the legs and antennae as desired.

Teacher Tips
- To make glue-paint, mix together equal amounts of glue and paint.
- Use a clothespin to hold the antennae in place while the glue dries.

Julie Koczur

Fireflies!

Bring the glow of these summer critters right into your classroom with this idea. After youngsters complete their projects, display them on a windowsill for all to admire.

Materials (per child)

- sheet of black or dark blue construction paper
- white tempera paint
- gold glitter glue
- fine-tipped black marker

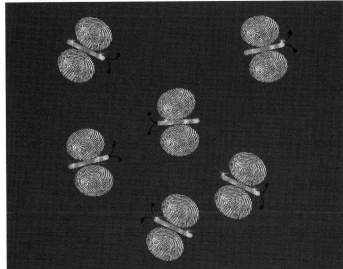

Directions

1. For each firefly, glue a short line of glitter on the construction paper.
2. When the glue is dry, use the white paint to print a fingerprint wing on each side of each firefly body.
3. When the paint is dry, add details with the marker.

GLITTER GLUE

Teacher Tips

- To make the wings appear lighter, have youngsters blot painted fingers on newspaper before printing.
- If desired, make the fireflies on a simple white jar cutout, using black ink pad fingerprints to make the wings.
- For math practice, ask each child to label his sky or jar with the number of fireflies in it. Place sets of three to five projects in your math center; then have youngsters arrange them in numerical order.

adapted from an idea by Alyssa Weller—Skokie, IL

Dazzling Dragonfly Pin

This dandy dragonfly is a gift giver's delight! Simply dazzling!

Materials (per child)

- mini craft stick
- 1½"-long pin backing
- blue, green, or purple tempera paint
- black craft foam
- blue and green glitter
- paintbrush
- ink pen
- permanent marker
- scissors
- craft glue

Directions

1. Use the pen to trace the craft stick twice onto the black foam. Cut out the shapes.
2. Paint the craft stick the color of your choice; then let the paint dry.
3. Glue the pin backing to one end of the craft stick. Glue the foam cutouts near the other end, forming an *X*, to resemble wings. Let the glue dry.
4. Brush a light coat of glue on the dragonfly's body and wings. Sprinkle a dusting of both glitter colors onto the glue.
5. After the glue dries, use the permanent marker to dot eyes on the dragonfly.

Teacher Tips
- For a more delicate look, use fine-textured glitter on the dragonfly.
- Use a clothespin to hold the wings in place while the glue dries.

Colleen Dabney—Williamsburg, VA

Buttermilk Chalk Drawings

Commemorate Dairy Month with this "moo-velous" art technique. After youngsters complete their pictures, how about a snack of buttermilk biscuits and jam?

Materials (per child)

- chalk in assorted colors
- buttermilk
- white typing paper
- plastic bowl
- colorful sheet of construction paper

Directions

1. Partially fill the bowl with buttermilk.
2. Dip the chalk color of your choice in the buttermilk.
3. Draw a design with the wet chalk on the white paper. Continue to dip the chalk as needed to keep the end wet.
4. Repeat Steps 2 and 3 for each desired chalk color.
5. Let the picture dry; then mount it on the construction paper.

Teacher Tip

- After use, rinse the chalk with water; then let it air-dry.

Alyssa Weller—Skokie, IL

Fourth of July Sparkler

July 4th celebrations will sparkle with these glittery party favors. Play some patriotic music; then invite youngsters to wave their sparklers as they march and move to the music.

Directions

1. Paint the tube and cap of the flower pick with glue-paint. Sprinkle glitter on the paint while it is still wet. Then let the paint dry.
2. Fit the end of the pick into the straw and secure with craft glue. Let the glue dry.
3. Twist the pipe cleaners together. Then fold the ends toward each other.
4. Poke the folded end of the pipe cleaners into the top of the pick. Bend and spread the pipe cleaners as desired.
5. Tie red, white, and blue ribbon around the sparkler. Then curl the ends of the ribbon.

Teacher Tips

- To make glue-paint, mix equal amounts of glue and blue paint.
- Poke the glittered flower pick into a foam cube to keep it upright while the glue-paint dries.

Mackie Rhodes—Greensboro, NC

Patriotic Placemat

Invite youngsters to pack these all-American placemats for their Fourth of July picnics. Encourage students to use their patriotic placemats for their meal, then wave them in flaglike fashion during the fireworks show. What a display of patriotism!

Materials (per child)

- several laminated tagboard stars (see Teacher Tip)
- white construction paper
- water-thinned blue paint in a spray bottle
- red and black permanent markers
- newspaper
- tape
- laminating machine

Directions

1. To make a mat, use rolled pieces of tape to lightly attach several stars to a sheet of white paper.
2. Spread out some newspaper; then place the white mat on it.
3. Spray the mat with blue paint. When the paint dries, gently remove the stars from the mat.
4. Use permanent markers to add patriotic decorations and lettering to the mat.
5. Laminate the decorated mat.

Teacher Tip
- To make tagboard stars, copy the star pattern on page 175 several times onto tagboard. Then cut out and laminate each star.

Colleen Dabney—Williamsburg, VA

Stars and Stripes Forever!

These patriotic pictures bring wonderful practice in cutting and creating. Here's to the red, white, and blue!

Materials (per child)

- stars (see Teacher Tips)
- red, white, dark blue, and light blue construction paper
- ruler
- pencil
- scissors
- glue

Directions

1. Use the pencil and ruler to draw stripes on the construction paper. Cut out the stripes.
2. Creatively arrange and glue the stripes onto a sheet of light blue paper.
3. Add stars to the collage.

Teacher Tips

- Provide red, blue, and/or white die-cut stars. Or copy reduced and enlarged star patterns (page 175) onto construction paper. Then, if abilities permit, have each child cut out his own stars.
- For extra pizzazz, cut stripes from paper decorated with patriotic designs, and cut the stars from blue holographic paper.

Linda Masternak Justice—Kansas City, MO

Sunshine Kid

This decorative magnet will bring a handful of sunshine into any parent's life. Encourage each child to give his project to a very special family member or friend.

Materials (per child)

- large sheet of white construction paper
- yellow tempera paint
- paintbrush
- photo of child
- plastic cup
- scissors
- glue
- magnetic tape
- permanent marker

You Are My Sunshine!

Directions

1. Paint your hand with yellow paint; then make handprints on the white paper to make a circle. (Add more paint as needed.)
2. When the paint is dry, cut out the sun (handprint circle).
3. Use a plastic cup to trace a circle around the photo; then cut it out.
4. Glue the photo in the center of the sun.
5. Use the marker to write "You Are My Sunshine!" on the sun.
6. Attach a piece of magnetic tape to the back of the project.

Teacher Tip

- If photos are not available, have each child use craft supplies to create a self-portrait to use instead.

Susan DeRiso—Barrington, RI
Jana Sanderson—Stockton, CA

Lemon Sun Visor

Youngsters can have fun in the sun while shading their eyes with these refreshing sun visors. And they make great props for summertime lemonade sellers!

Materials (per child)

- one-half of a 9" paper plate
- 1½" x 18" yellow construction paper strip
- yellow, light yellow, and white tempera paint (see Teacher Tip)
- teardrop-shaped sponge
- cotton swab
- paintbrush
- scissors
- stapler

Directions

1. Paint the back of the plate yellow. Let the paint dry.
2. Sponge-paint several light yellow teardrop shapes on the plate so that it resembles a crosscut view of a lemon.
3. Use the cotton swab to paint a few white seeds on the lemon.
4. When the paint is dry, staple a yellow paper headband to the lemon, adjusting the length to fit the child's head.

Teacher Tip
● To make light yellow paint, mix a small amount of yellow paint with white paint.

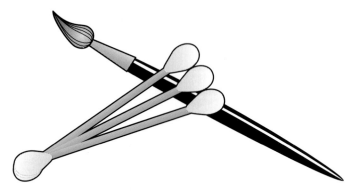

Susan DeRiso—Barrington, RI

Cool Card

Invite each child to make this cool summer-time greeting card. She might use it for a Father's Day card or any other seasonal occasion. Cool!

Materials (per child)

- light blue construction paper copy of card pattern (page 176)
- flexible drinking straw
- lemon half (see Teacher Tips)
- yellow paint
- scissors
- paintbrush
- markers
- glue

Directions

1. Cut out the card.
2. Brush a light coat of yellow paint onto the lemon half; then make lemon prints on the card. Apply paint to the lemon as often as needed.
3. When the paint is dry, fold the card in half. Use the markers to write a message inside.
4. Glue the straw into the fold so that the elbow extends just above the card.

Teacher Tips
- To reduce the amount of juice produced by the lemon, allow it to air-dry for several hours before use.
- Use a clothespin to hold the straw in place while the glue dries.

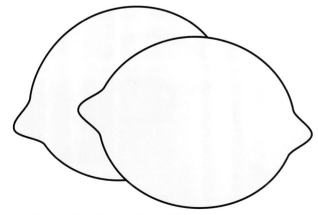

Amy Barsanti—Plymouth, NC

Pocket Pet

Youngsters will enjoy collecting small treasures with these special friends. Just have each child deposit her finds into her container, snap on the lid, and slip her pet into a pocket.

Materials (per child)

- lidded film canister
- 1" pom-pom and 5 small pom-poms in matching colors
- craft foam to match pom-pom color
- 3 black mini pom-poms
- black yarn
- scissors
- craft glue

Directions

1. Cut out a pair of cat or dog ears from craft foam.
2. To make your pet's head, glue the ears, mini pom-pom eyes and nose, and yarn mouth onto the large pom-pom. Let the glue dry.
3. Glue the head and the small pom-poms onto the canister (as shown) to make your pet's body.

Teacher Tip
- To make your pet sit up, glue the head to the lid as shown above.

Mackie Rhodes—Greensboro, NC

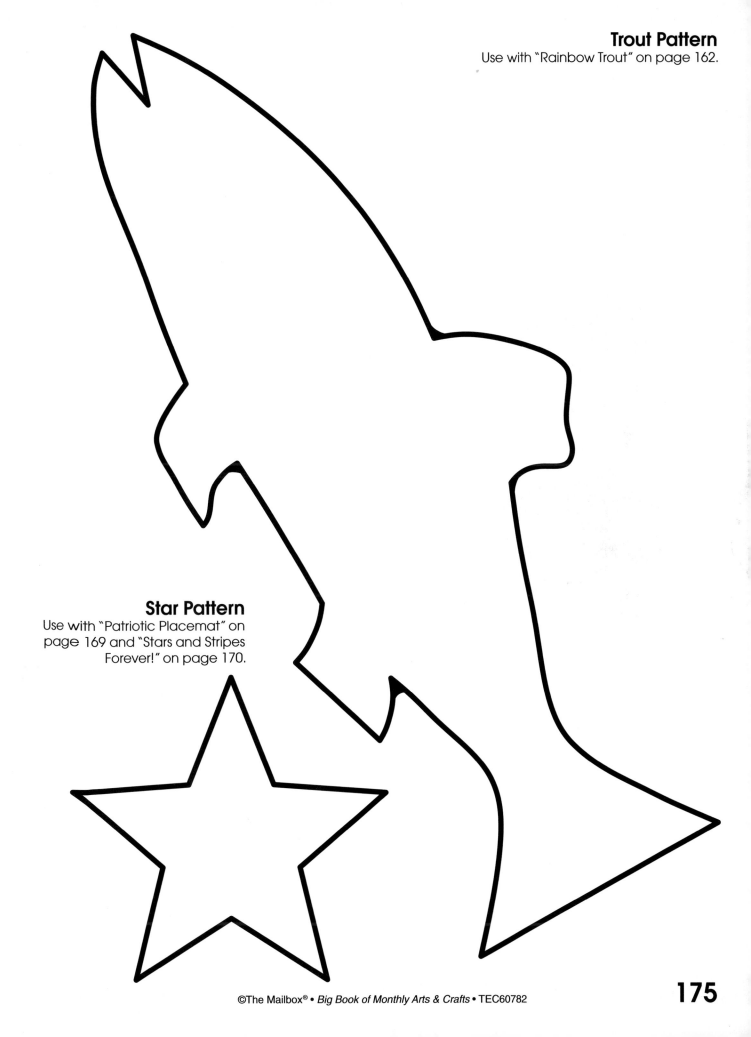

Star Pattern
Use with "Patriotic Placemat" on page 169 and "Stars and Stripes Forever!" on page 170.

Card Pattern
Use with "Cool Card" on page 173.

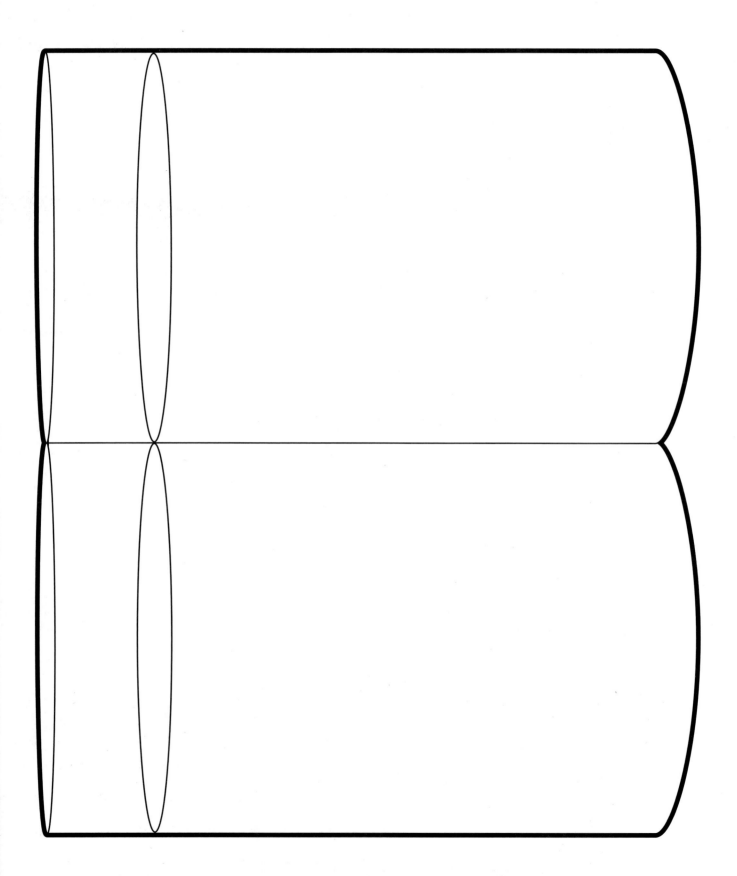

176